The Little Bitcoin Book

Why Bitcoin Matters for Your Freedom, Finances, and Future

Timi Ajiboye

Luis Buenaventura

Alex Gladstein

Lily Liu

Alexander Lloyd

Alejandro Machado

Jimmy Song

Alena Vranova

Published by 21 Million Books
Redwood City, CA

Book design and illustrations by Luis Buenaventura.
"Venezuelan blockade" illustration by Timi Ajiboye.

First Edition (Ed. 01-201909191303)

ISBN 978-1-64199-050-9

Contents

Foreword

We are activists, educators, entrepreneurs, executives, investors, and researchers. We are from Africa, Asia, Europe, North America, and South America. We differ in many ways, but are all fascinated by Bitcoin and the impact we believe it will have on our world and in our lives.

In March 2019, Jimmy talked to some of us about the idea of doing a book sprint, where we would come together in an isolated location for a few days to write a book about Bitcoin and its importance for society. Two months later, at the Oslo Freedom Forum, we gathered on a rooftop in Norway, surrounded by the excited hum of human rights activists and journalists from all continents. The conversation inevitably turned to Bitcoin and its world-changing possibilities. Alex encouraged the group to write a book explaining why Bitcoin matters without using the technobabble that is so common in books of this genre. We wanted to help the curious person understand the human impact of one of the most profound innovations of our time. A few months later, the eight of us met in a house in California to make this idea a reality.

What you now hold in your hands is the result of that four-day effort. The goal of this book is to help you understand why there are problems with today's monetary system, why Bitcoin was invented to provide an alternative, how it will change politics and society, and what it means for the future.

We sincerely hope that as you read this book, you will become as awestruck by Bitcoin as we are.

August 8, 2019
Redwood City, California

About the Authors

Timi Ajiboye is a software developer and entrepreneur based in Lagos, Nigeria. He co-founded and currently runs BuyCoins (buycoins.africa), an exchange that lets Africans easily buy and sell bitcoin with their local currency. Twitter: @timigod

Luis Buenaventura is a co-founder at BloomX (bloom.solutions), a startup in the Philippines that's bringing safe cryptocurrency trading to the emerging world. A prolific speaker and author, he's also the creator of Cryptopop.net, an art initiative that's making crypto more accessible to the mainstream. Twitter: @helloluis

Alex Gladstein is the Chief Strategy Officer of the Human Rights Foundation (hrf.org), a non-profit that promotes civil liberties and challenges authoritarianism around the world. He also lectures about Bitcoin and governance for Singularity University, and has written about the intersection of technology and freedom in outlets like TIME, CNN, and Bitcoin Magazine. Twitter: @gladstein

Lily Liu is an investor and entrepreneur. Most recently she was co-founder and CFO of Earn.com, a platform that allowed you to earn bitcoin in your free time, which was sold to Coinbase in 2018. Prior to that, she built a hospital in China, worked at KKR and McKinsey, and studied at Stanford and Harvard. Twitter: @calilyliu

Alexander Lloyd has been investing in early-stage startups since 1998 and in 2008 he founded Accelerator Ventures. His first job was at Goldman Sachs in currency trading. In 2016, he joined the board of the Human Rights Foundation, where he focuses on North Korea. Twitter: @alex01

Alejandro Machado is a founder of the Open Money Initiative (openmoneyinitiative.org), a non-profit that researches how people use money in closed economies and collapsing monetary systems. He's focused on improving access to digital money for Venezuelans. Twitter: @alegw

Jimmy Song is a Bitcoin developer, educator, and entrepreneur. He's the author of Programming Bitcoin (programmingbitcoin.com), published by O'Reilly. He's focused on bringing sound money to the world. Jimmy's cowboy hat color is indicative of whether he plans to be nice or mean. His PGP fingerprint is C1D7 97BE 7D10 5291 228C D70C FAA6 17E3 2679 E455. Twitter: @jimmysong

Alena Vranova has developed successful financial service businesses since 2003. For the past 7 years she's been helping individuals and small businesses protect their bitcoins with non-custodial products and services. In 2013 she introduced Trezor, the first bitcoin hardware wallet, and she currently heads strategy at Casa (keys.casa), making personal bitcoin security and financial sovereignty accessible to everyone. Twitter: @AlenaSatoshi

The authors on Day 3 of the book sprint.

CHAPTER ONE
What's Wrong with Money Today?

The year is 1981.

In Manila, a young Filipino couple welcomes their first child into the world just months after martial law is officially lifted for the first time in a decade. The dictator Ferdinand Marcos will stay in power for a few more years, but for now, Luis' parents are concerned only for their young family's well-being. They have a small savings account and have begun putting money away in earnest for the first time, preparing for the turbulent years ahead. The exchange rate is seven Philippine pesos for one US dollar.

The year is 1993.

In Lagos, the Nigerian General Sani Abacha seizes power and fixes one US dollar to 22 Nigerian naira. It is an aggressive move that attempts to stabilize the economy by preventing the naira from further decline. The pegged exchange rate gives rise to a vibrant underground economy where naira trade at a much lower value. At the time of Abacha's death in 1998, dollars change hands on the black market for as much as 88 naira, four times the official government rate. Millions suffer as they can no longer afford the rising prices of food on their static government salaries.

The year is 2018.

Everywhere along the porous border of Venezuela, citizens flee the country's record-breaking 400,000% hyperinflation by crossing into neighboring Colombia and Brazil. More than 3 million have already escaped from the devastating starvation and social breakdown.

Lorena, a 48-year-old baker, makes the difficult decision to cross into Colombia. At the border, guards search her belongings, looking for valuables to confiscate. They find nothing. They don't know that Lorena spent hours beforehand carefully rolling US dollar bills around bobby pins and hiding them in her elaborate braids. She strides into a new country, head held high.

In Manila, Luis' parents see their luck turn for the worse. The exchange rate is now 50 Philippine pesos for one US dollar, and their patient saving over the years has resulted in an overall loss of more than 80% of their wealth. With their retirement imminent, they have no choice but to continue working and saving for an unforgiving and unpredictable future.

In Lagos, the naira is in a brief period of relative stability after losing another 50% against the dollar in just a few years. Prices of local goods have skyrocketed again. No one trusts that the government can prevent another economic crisis, not even the government officials themselves.

The year is 2019.

In Shanghai, a young professional named Annie messages one of her friends on WeChat, the popular social media platform used daily by more than a billion Chinese. Her friend mentions that he's in trouble for smoking marijuana, and in the middle of their chat conversation, he suddenly stops responding.

The next day, a pair of plainclothes police officers visit Annie at her office and ask her to come with them. Her colleagues see her leave and she disappears for several weeks. When she finally comes back online, she has lost some of her WeChat's payment features. She can no longer buy plane or train tickets. Her credit score plummets. Her life is ruined by a single string of text messages.

In Oakland, Alex walks into a pet store looking for dog food. He finds what he's looking for, plus an interesting new product, one that promises to make his dog's breath smell better. He swipes his Chase Visa card to pay for the food and walks out. A few minutes later, he checks Twitter, and an advertisement pops up for dog treats exactly like the ones he just bought. He discovers that Chase shares information about his daily payments with third party companies.

Alex realizes that details of his personal life are being handed over to advertisers with an unsettling feeling all too familiar to those in the smartphone generation. Even in the US, financial privacy is disappearing.

These are stories about how money is broken.

Luis's parents and millions of others in the Filipino and Nigerian middle class watched their savings evaporate in slow motion over a single generation. Lorena needed a way to carry her meager savings to a new home in Colombia without confiscation, so she got creative with her hairstyle. Annie is now in "financial jail" in China because one of her friends smoked pot. Alex's purchases are monitored and resold to numerous corporations with each swipe of his credit card.

These cases are not unique.

Since 2000, nearly all currencies have lost significant value against the US dollar. Many, such as the South African rand, Argentine peso, and Turkish lira have lost nearly 50%. An unfortunate handful like the Ukrainian hryvnia and the Dominican peso have lost as much as 70%. Even the US dollar and euro have lost 33% of their purchasing power in that time.

Around the world, 250 million migrants and refugees struggle to send their money home or take it with them to new frontiers. Some two billion people don't have access to a bank account or lack the official state identification required to get one. In an increasingly globalized world, money remains stubbornly local.

Meanwhile, in supercities like Shanghai and San Francisco the disconcerting feeling of being observed is palpable. For one thing, Big Brother is watching. For another, surveillance capitalism tracks every purchase and sells that data to dozens of companies without the purchaser's permission. Privacy is now a luxury, one whose price appears to be getting higher with each passing day.

What Is Money?

At its core, money is a social agreement.

Money requires people to trust that the bills in their wallets, the digits in their bank accounts, and the balances on their gift cards are all redeemable in the future for things that they want or need. The seller needs to agree that the buyer's money is valuable.

Throughout history, societies have experimented with various ways to conduct this agreement, using everything from seashells, salt, and gold to the complex central banking systems in use today. Some kinds of money are more sound than others, meaning that they hold their value better over time.

Instinctively, everyone knows that money matters and that they want to have the soundest money possible. Because most people exchange their labor for money, it comes to represent a person's time and effort. Money is the medium through which labor is converted into goods and services in the present and future. In this sense, access to sound money is one of the most enduring forms of personal power.

Money also matters immensely for government. Because today's economies are organized by nation-states, governments hold the power to control money. However, the control of money can be a tempting thing to abuse. Officials often manipulate this power to suit their interests. Only the most democratic governments, which protect individual rights, separation of powers, and the rule of law, can effectively guard against monetary abuse such as runaway inflation, arbitrary confiscation, and corruption.

How Does Modern Money Work?

All national currencies in circulation today are called *fiat* currencies, which is Latin for "by decree." The value of these currencies is set by the decree of the nation-states that issue and accept them. Since governments can create more fiat currency at little cost, it is possible to print new units of currency ad infinitum whenever they choose.

Alan Greenspan, former chairman of the US Federal Reserve, famously said that the US can "pay any debt that it has because we can always print money to do that." This practice can cause problems, even in the world's most stable economies. The oldest national currency is the United Kingdom's Pound Sterling, which has lost 99.5% of its purchasing power over the last 300 years. The US dollar has lost 90% of its purchasing power in just the last century. A steak that cost $0.36 in 1925 was $3 in the 1990s and costs $12 today. And these are some of the most stable fiat currencies to ever exist. The average fiat currency has a lifespan of just 27 years.

Low and stable inflation is the goal of modern central banks, and there have been varying periods of success depending on the country. However, most currencies suffer from high inflation over the long term, which can be devastating to savings. This is especially true for those who are unable to afford hard assets, like real estate or blue chip stocks, whose values rise with inflation. High inflation can make it difficult for all but the wealthy to save for the future.

For billions of people who live under authoritarian regimes, the value of their savings diminishes due to the decisions of unelected government officials. Only the elite are typically able to access dollars, gold, or real estate to preserve value. Meanwhile, citizens in wealthy democracies enjoy some important protections. They have easy access to a relatively stable currency like the dollar or euro. Their economies tend to perform well, so they're more likely to have a job that pays well over time. They also have access to a range of investment products to offset or outpace inflation.

The effect of the elite disproportionately benefiting from newly printed money is so prevalent that there's a term for it: the Cantillon Effect. It is named after Richard Cantillon, an 18th-century economist who noticed this effect while working as a banker in the UK. Dramatic or large-scale inflation can be an unfair way of distributing wealth as it inevitably benefits the already-haves at the expense of the have-nots. And while its effects may not be evident to the average person in the United States or the United Kingdom, they are painfully felt by billions of citizens in countries with less stable economies.

Fiat money systems have also been enablers of the prolonged wars of the modern age. Governments can print more money for war, distributing cost to future generations via inflation.

This means longer and more expensive wars. World War I is a tragic example, as the main actors funded the later stages of the wars with inflation. Both Russia and Germany suspended the *gold standard*, where their fiat currencies were convertible to a fixed amount of gold. Instead, they suspended the convertibility and printed money with no backing to continue fighting. As a result, the war ended up lasting much longer than anyone thought possible. When Germany lost, the only way they could pay the huge reparations was by printing even more money. By 1923, the Deutsche mark depreciated to one-trillionth of its pre-war value, setting the stage for World War II.

Similar profligate spending is evident in recent times as well. Regardless of what one might think about the US military involvement in Afghanistan and Iraq, the costs of these invasions are in excess of $5.9 trillion. This comes out to more than $46,000 per household if the American taxpayer had been asked to finance the war directly.

Another issue of the modern money system is that it can be extremely difficult to move money between different nations around the world. Governments in countries like China, Russia, Argentina, and Indonesia have aggressively restricted how much money their citizens are allowed to exchange, transfer, or take abroad.

This is done primarily by controlling each individual's ability to exchange their local currency for foreign ones like the US dollar. The average Chinese national, for instance, is only allowed to convert up to $50,000 of their renminbi every year.

In other parts of the world, even the ability to access one's own money locally can be severely limited. After their 2015 financial crisis, Greek citizens were restricted from withdrawing more than 60 euros per day from their bank accounts, a stark reminder that they didn't control their money.

Even when people can send money abroad, it is cumbersome and costly. In 2018, migrant workers and refugees sent nearly $700 billion across borders in remittances to support their loved ones. Exchange rates and tariffs consumed $45 billion of that money, a massive amount for those who don't have money to spare.

A Global Single Point of Failure

All central banks represent a single point of failure for their national economies. The US Federal Reserve acts, in a way, as a central bank for all the world's banks. For Americans, this arrangement seems to function very well. The dollar is accepted everywhere, and it is easy for most people to open bank accounts, get credit lines, and pay for goods and services. Most Americans don't suffer noticeably from inflation.

The dynamic US economy helps underpin and fuel today's global economic system. At its heart is the *dollar standard*, a global monetary hegemony that began with a little-known event at a New Hampshire hotel in 1944 called the Bretton Woods Agreement.

Global powers hosted a gathering at Bretton Woods to establish a unifying monetary order as World War II drew to a close. For three weeks, more than 700 delegates from 44 countries debated and negotiated the structure of the future financial system. Some delegates suggested the creation of a new international reserve currency called the *bancor*. In the end, the delegates agreed that their currencies would be pegged to the US dollar. As a result, international trade today is primarily settled in dollars, and every country tries to maintain a reserve of dollars.

The central nature of the US dollar to the global economic system is revealed in the way that money moves between countries. Take for example sending money from South Korea to the Philippines. It is not usually possible for Korean won to be exchanged directly for Philippine pesos because the two countries don't keep enough of each other's currencies on hand. Instead, they rely on the dollar and a series of transactions. First, Korean won is sold for dollars in Seoul. Those dollars are transferred from a South Korean bank to a Filipino one via a US bank. Finally, the bank in Manila converts the dollars to Philippine pesos. This takes at least a few days and incurs foreign exchange and transaction fees which can range from a few percent for popular routes to low double digits for less popular ones. The global average cost for these kind of cross-border payments remains at over 7%, even for small remittances.

While the world has benefited in many ways from having the dollar standard, it has also resulted in a fragility whereby every economy relies in some way on the US dollar and is vulnerable to its collapse. This results in a system where a handful of bank failures in the US can lead to global economic catastrophe.

The End of Financial Privacy

The digitization of money over the last two decades has resulted in ever-diminishing levels of personal privacy, with each transaction now being exploited for political control and commercial potential. Electronic money has existed for a long time, but only recently has the big data analysis necessary to effectively conduct mass surveillance been possible. Neither online nor physical purchases are safe, as governments and advertisers increasingly tap into profiles of each individual's preferences, decisions, and connections. These profiles are like data footprints, unique to each person, and become more refined and easily identifiable with each new purchase. This has led to a world in which a Google search for a product can result in Facebook and Instagram advertisements for that same product minutes later.

Depending on one's location, personal digital footprints can have dangerous repercussions. In the summer of 2019, students in Hong Kong banded together by the tens of thousands to protest a newly proposed law that would allow the Chinese government to extradite anyone to Beijing without due process. They knew that if they used their student ID-linked *Octopus cards* to navigate the metro system their locations would be betrayed, so instead, they used cash to buy one-time use tickets. This is a safe option for now, but paper and metal money are on track to be phased out of most major urban areas over the next decade. At that point, there will be no way to use public transit systems without revealing one's personal location to the authorities and corporations. Digital footprints will be everywhere.

The public reaction to corporate and government tracking of citizens' spending behavior ranges. Some simply find it unsettling, others decry it as a major violation of privacy, while most don't seem to care at all. Either way, the fact is that beyond controlling the money supply and where money can be sent, authorities can now learn virtually everything about buyers and sellers. The world's increasingly digital payment systems could usher in the extinction of personal privacy.

Is There Another Way?

Four global phenomena — the devaluation of personal wealth, the restriction of value transfer, financial centralization, and the loss of privacy — represent major risks to the individual as they navigate the 21st century monetary system.

People around the world are feeling the pressure as countries struggle to maintain the status quo.

What if a new system emerged in which governments did not have the ability to arbitrarily devalue money, and faceless corporations couldn't freeze user funds or refuse to process transactions? What if money were entirely digital, able to be used by anyone with internet access from anywhere on earth, without needing to ask permission from the authorities?

In the wake of the 2008 financial crisis, someone decided to build exactly such a system, setting the stage for the next great financial revolution.

CHAPTER TWO
What is Bitcoin?

On September 15, 2008, the renowned investment bank Lehman Brothers filed for the largest bankruptcy in US history. The collapse of Lehman Brothers, founded in 1850, was the culmination of a global borrowing binge. The company had risked far more that the total value of the firm on mortgaged backed securities, including many risky subprime loans. When homeowners stopped making mortgage payments, the firm became insolvent and was unable to recover.

Suddenly, the trust that banks had established in Lehman Brothers and in one another evaporated. Amidst this credit crunch, businesses found it difficult to take out loans to finance their activities. With no funds to buy inventory, invest in new equipment, or pay employees, companies in many industries looked like they wouldn't be able to continue operating. A vicious downward spiral appeared imminent.

The US Treasury and the Federal Reserve acted quickly to stave off economic doom by loaning banks money to keep the financial system afloat. On October 3, 2008, Congress bailed out several troubled banks with the Emergency Economic Stabilization Act of 2008. The government spent hundreds of billions of dollars to shore up a collapsing financial sector.

Enter Bitcoin

On October 31, 2008, a few weeks after the US government authorized $700 billion to bail out the banks, an unknown person or group of people going by the name of Satoshi Naka-moto released a technical *whitepaper* outlining a new electronic payment system called Bitcoin. Satoshi presented the white-paper to an internet mailing list of cryptography researchers called the cypherpunks — a group of privacy activists who create tools for challenging surveillance and the abuse of state power.

The whitepaper had two significant points of intrigue. First, the author chose to use a pseudonym. Satoshi's identity remains a mystery of popular interest to this day. Second, the paper introduced something that had never existed before: digital money that did not rely on a central authority. Few thought a breakthrough of this kind was even possible.

A few months later, Satoshi launched the Bitcoin network and left a clue as to why in a single line of text, embedded in the first entry of Bitcoin's accounting ledger:

*The Times 03/Jan/2009 Chancellor on brink of
second bailout for banks*

This referred to a headline that appeared on January 3, 2009 in *The Times*, a prominent UK newspaper. Satoshi's message to the world was that the current system, where banks were rescued at the expense of the people, was broken. Bitcoin's new decentralized financial technology was built to be a way out.

To understand the scientific innovation behind Bitcoin, it is first essential to understand scarcity.

The Two Types of Scarcity

In the physical realm, there are two forms of scarcity. The first is human-made and in that sense, artificial: collectibles like Limited Edition Chanel handbags, Michael Jordan basketball cards, rare vintages of wine, or numbered works of art from a particular artist. This is also called *centralized* scarcity. Notice that these items tend to have counterfeit problems.

The second kind of scarcity is natural. This category includes salt (the origin for the word salary), glass beads from Ghana, seashells from Native American culture, silver from China, and of course gold throughout the world. These are examples of *decentralized* scarcity and tend to be harder to counterfeit.

It is no coincidence that decentralized, scarce commodities like salt and gold have been used as money. First, there's a fairness in using a commodity that no single person or group controls. Second, these commodities are much harder to counterfeit. Lastly, the scarcity helps keep the economic transactions easy to conduct as there isn't a need to carry unreasonable amounts of it to buy something.

What differentiates the two different forms of scarcity is control. Centralized scarcity is created by one company or person — whether it be the People's Bank of China, the Federal Reserve, an artist, or a large multinational corporation. That entity, or *central authority*, fully controls the scarcity of a commodity through creating, issuing, buying back, and confiscating.

Decentralized scarce commodities are created by nature, meaning that there's no central authority that makes the commodity. There is no crafting, rather, the process is more akin to collecting or harvesting. To mine a naturally scarce commodity like gold or oil, a miner extracts what already exists from the ground.

In the case of gold, its accumulation hasn't historically needed permission from anyone other than the owner of a mining site. In other words, there is no center from which all gold begins its life and no global authority empowered to restrict mining or increase the supply.

This is the key distinction between centralized and decentralized scarce commodities, particularly ones that are used as money.

Why Decentralization Can Be a Good Thing for Money

As mentioned earlier, one of the inescapable features of centralized money is that the creator can arbitrarily inflate the supply, printing more on a whim. While this is done much more often and to a much greater extent by authoritarian regimes than by democracies, it is something that occurs in all societies.

In the movie *Bugsy,* the title character sells paper shares of the Pink Flamingo casino to investors over and over again. To each person he sells 20% of the casino for $10,000. He does this with more than a dozen investors, misrepresenting how much of the casino they have purchased. Each investor assumes he or she now owns 20% of the casino, but actually owns much less. Bugsy, however, benefits, since he gets a lot more money.

Every centralized commodity faces the same problem of incentives. The central authority can create more of the commodity, diluting the value for all other owners. Central banks that print more money usually do so with positive goals like building infrastructure, supporting social welfare programs, or stabilizing an economic crisis. However, recall the Cantillon Effect from Chapter 1: even reasonable use of this power can result in benefits for the rich and powerful at the expense of the poor and powerless. The ability to print money creates a moral hazard.

Of course, dilution can happen to decentralized money as well. New technology can make the collection of a rare naturally-occuring commodity cheaper, and as a result the market can get flooded with new supply. Once a commodity loses its scarcity, it becomes much weaker and less sound. This is why salt and seashells and glass beads are no longer used as money. Each used to be hard to gather at scale, but their collection is now extremely easy and cheap because of technological innovation.

Gold is one of the few exceptions and continues to hold its value remarkably well even after thousands of years of mining. While gold has some industrial and decorative uses, its historical mining difficulty has meant a relatively sound money whose stable purchasing power has made it a very good store of value. Even today, gold jewelry is used in some countries as a way to hedge against economic crises. Gold's primary disadvantage is its physicality and weight, as storage, security, and transfer can be challenging.

Many proponents of Bitcoin believe it may eventually replace gold as the preferred store of value for long-term savings. As this Chapter will show, it is decentralized and more scarce than gold, but also far easier to transport and securely store.

Decentralized Digital Scarcity

With the advent of the internet, information could finally be digitized and distributed on a wide scale. Copying a digital file is much easier and cheaper than replicating something in the physical world.

The digitization of money was a necessary innovation for e-commerce, eliminating the need for physical transfer. Everything can be sent at the speed of email or a web page load, which reduces friction and enables trade to be truly global. Digital versions of fiat money are created by banks, and then processed by credit card networks (Visa, MasterCard), retail companies (Alibaba, Amazon, Apple), and even internet-native payment processors (WeChat, PayPal, Square).

Since they are the sole arbiters of how their money is used, all these companies can censor transactions. They can seize money and close accounts, and oftentimes do so without customer consent. What's more, since they are centralized structures, these companies are often the target of government pressure or even hacking attacks which can result in the loss of customer funds or data. Before Bitcoin, this was the inevitable tradeoff for digital money: it had to be artificially scarce, or controlled by central authorities. There didn't seem to be a way to create scarcity in the digital realm.

Satoshi Nakamoto revealed a breakthrough on October 31, 2008, by presenting Bitcoin as a new digital currency whose scarcity is rooted in the fact that there are scarce items in the digital realm: rare numbers.

Some of the rarest numbers are prime numbers. A prime, like 2, 3, or 5, can only be divided by 1 and itself.

Primes get increasingly rare as numbers get bigger. For example, between 1 and 100, there are 25 prime numbers. You might then expect there to be 250 primes between 1 and 1,000, but there are only 168. Primes become incredibly scarce after 100 billion, so much so that there continues to be a global mathematical search underway for the largest prime number.

In the Bitcoin network, the production of new bitcoins occurs through a global competition where participants search for rare numbers much like prime numbers. This enables decentralized scarcity in the digital realm. This is what makes Satoshi's invention so profound. Every asset before Bitcoin was either totally centralized (World of Warcraft gold), physical (silver), or infinitely abundant (MP3s). A decentralized, digital, *and* scarce asset simply did not exist before Bitcoin.

Bitcoin Mining: Decentralized Payment Processing

Bitcoin's decentralized nature is based on the fact that it is a scarce natural commodity like gold and is hard to mine. Much like gold mining, Bitcoin mining is the search for something very rare in the midst of the much more common. Once a Bitcoin miner finds the right rare number it can be cheaply and easily be verified by others and just like gold can be relatively easily distinguished from fool's gold.

Instead of using pickaxes and excavation machines to search for gold, bitcoin miners use powerful computers to search for particular rare numbers. Once found, each rare number is called a *proof-of-work* because it *proves* to everyone that a lot of work went into finding it.

As with gold, no permission from a central authority is required to mine: anyone can download mining software to start searching for rare numbers that fit the criteria.

Even better than gold mining, there is no special type of land required, just computer equipment and an affordable power source. As a result, miners around the world search independently in a competition to find proof-of-work that meet the criteria required by the Bitcoin network.

Thus, Bitcoin runs without a single point of failure. Contrast this with centralized systems. If the Visa network goes down, no one can pay for anything with their Visa cards. The same would happen with Paypal or Amazon if their respective networks went down. Unlike these companies, Bitcoin has no central authority or single point of failure. No one can choose to censor a particular transaction. Bitcoin's unstoppable network of miners provide a critical service, processing transactions without the vulnerabilities of a central authority.

How Bitcoin Transactions Work

So how do Bitcoin transactions work?

To understand this, consider something that's probably more familiar: a bank's ledger system. After someone writes a check to pay for a good or service, the recipient goes to their bank to deposit the check. Assuming both customers have an account at this bank, the bank only has to debit the sender's account and credit the receiver's account. The whole process requires adding only two entries in the bank's accounting ledger. Bank officials don't go into a vault, take the exact amount out of the sender's stash of coins and bills and then put it into the receiver's stash of coins and bills. Accounting using a ledger was a key historical invention that made the transfer of money much less laborious. The equivalent of a bank check in bitcoin is a *transaction*.

Bitcoin operates a special kind of ledger called a *blockchain*. Thousands of people running Bitcoin validation software check the blockchain continuously instead of a central authority. Each person running the software keeps a copy of the entire ledger and verifies the new entries. This is called running a *full node*. Each full node constantly checks to enforce the same rules of Bitcoin, and in this way, no central authority can arbitrarily edit the records to steal bitcoin or spend bitcoin they don't have. Bitcoin's blockchain is known as a *public blockchain* because anyone can look at the record of transactions.

Bitcoin owners carry out transactions in the same way that they might write a check. They specify the amount and then sign the check. But instead of scrawling their names on an easily forged piece of paper, bitcoin owners sign their transactions with a *digital signature* using cryptography.

This digital signature is created using a secret only known to the owner of the bitcoins. That secret is called a *private key*.

With the private key, the sender can make a digital signature that proves to the receiver that the sender owns the bitcoins.

Users store their bitcoins in a *wallet*, which is software run on a computer, phone, or specialized hardware. Every second, new Bitcoin transactions are initiated from wallets around the world, but there is no central payment processor. Instead, miners from around the world compete to record transactions into the ledger. They run their computing equipment and try to find a particular rare number. Every 10 minutes or so, a Bitcoin miner somewhere in the world finds proof-of-work and combines it into a *block* with a group of transactions that have been waiting to be processed. The miner then submits this block to the Bitcoin network for validation.

Each block is like a new page in Bitcoin's global ledger, and full nodes on the network verify that the transactions contained within are valid. Anyone can run a full node, so thousands of users are constantly verifying the validity of each new block. If the network confirms that a miner's proposed block is valid, then the miner receives a reward of 12.5 new bitcoins, and the block and all the transactions contained in it become a permanent part of Bitcoin history. As of this writing, a typical Bitcoin transaction takes less than an hour to be finalized on the blockchain.

Bitcoin's blockchain gets its name from the fact that it is the collection of all blocks, or all pages, in the historical ledger. In other words, the blockchain is the entire, immutable ledger of all transactions on the Bitcoin network since it was created in January 2009.

There are thousands of full nodes which make up the Bitcoin network. Each full node independently validates the newly proposed blocks from miners. The fairly modest hardware requirements mean that most modern laptops can run a Bitcoin full node. Since running full nodes remains relatively cheap and affordable, the network remains decentralized.

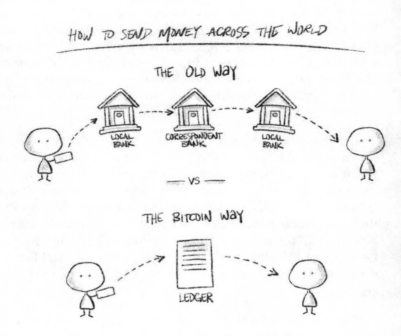

Bitcoin's Monetary Policy

Unlike the current system of central banking, which is opaque and constantly changing, Bitcoin's monetary policy is transparent and set in stone.

How do new bitcoins get issued? As mentioned, a miner who finds a valid proof-of-work and pairs it with a group of valid transactions — making a valid new block — is entitled to what's called the block reward. As of this writing, the block reward is 12.5 bitcoins and halves every four years, meaning that the reward will be 6.25 bitcoins in 2020, 3.125 bitcoins in 2024, and so on.

If a miner tries to cheat and claim a reward in excess of the scheduled block reward, that block is rejected by all of the full nodes verifying the block. Full nodes check all proposed blocks and any that don't follow the rules are not put into their blockchains. This is similar to when a bank rejects a check that overdraws from the sending account. As a result, no one can forge fake bitcoins. Any fraudulent transaction that tries to spend bitcoins that don't exist and any blocks that contain such transactions will be rejected by full nodes.

An invalid block is costly to miners, as it gets rejected and the large amount of electricity that they spent running their computing equipment to find the proof-of-work is wasted. This makes fraud very expensive and protects the Bitcoin network. Still, if there were only a few full nodes on the Bitcoin network, a miner might be able to get a fraudulent block into the blockchain by bribing those few full nodes. Since there are many thousands of full nodes on the network, and since they are geographically scattered and unknown to each other, such a strategy is almost guaranteed to fail.

Satoshi set the total supply of all bitcoin from inception at 21 million. Today, more than 85% of all bitcoins have already been mined, meaning more than 17 million are now in circulation. The rest will be released as rewards for miners in smaller and smaller chunks on a publicly-known schedule.

Blockchain Technology: Still Waiting

Many have tried to replicate the success of Satoshi's invention. A popular strategy is to take Bitcoin's blockchain ledger system and apply it to other use cases. Since 2014, many well-known companies have tried to use a blockchain in various industries, pouring many millions of dollars into the effort. This has generated a lot of hype and media attention around *blockchain technology*.

Unfortunately, most of these attempts so far are comparable to using a forklift for grocery shopping. The vehicle works perfectly well within its original context (storing the ledger for decentralized digital money), but appears to be too slow, unnecessarily wasteful, or non-functional for other applications (i.e. healthcare on the blockchain, tracking fruit on the blockchain, putting weather data on the blockchain, etc.).

Bitcoin is a combination of four important components, of which the blockchain is just one. The first is that bitcoin is a scarce digital asset. The second is that bitcoin is a peer-to-peer network of full nodes that can't be shut down or censored. The third is that mining Bitcoin requires finding valid proof-of-work numbers, making fraud very costly. The fourth is that Bitcoin has a blockchain that's fully and publicly auditable. These four technologies are tightly integrated, and when one part is removed, the result is something far less useful.

For a purely digital asset like Bitcoin, using a blockchain as a public record works. Both its creation and every instance of its transfer is perfectly recorded and infallible. But for real-world objects like coffee beans or healthcare data, there is no way to guarantee that the information is infallible, since there is always the possibility of mistakes made during data entry due to negligence, or even outright fraud. A central authority must therefore be present to vouch for all the information, which obviates the need for a blockchain in the first place.

Nevertheless, huge sums of money have been poured into blockchain technology in search of use cases beyond decentralized money. As of this writing, no one has been able to create a large-scale record-keeping system using a blockchain that significantly improves upon or even achieves parity with more traditional approaches.

What about other Cryptocurrencies?

People haven't just tried to copy Bitcoin's blockchain; they have also tried to create other cryptocurrencies, so called because senders of these new digital monies use digital signatures to sign transactions, just like Bitcoin. Often called altcoins or tokens, these projects aren't decentralized, and many are outright scams. Bitconnect is a famous example of cryptocurrency fraud.

A handful of cryptocurrencies may have legitimate use cases. These include Monero (XMR) and Zcash (ZEC), which aim to allow users to transact in a more private way than Bitcoin, or Ethereum (ETH), which is used to try and build blockchain application platforms. Major companies are also experimenting with cryptocurrencies. Facebook has announced the Libra cryptocurrency, which has the potential to become very popular due to the billions of people who use Facebook's services. However, Libra is centralized by nature and won't have Bitcoin's censorship-resistance and scarcity.

Several groups have tried to copy Satoshi's success in an especially brazen fashion and have created cryptocurrencies whose names contain the word Bitcoin. As such, there's often confusion about which cryptocurrency is actually Bitcoin. To distinguish, look for the ticker symbol BTC on exchanges and wallets. Variants of Bitcoin are like fool's gold; they may seem similar but are much more centralized and have a much lower price. These include *Bitcoin Cash* (BCH), *Bitcoin Gold* (BTG), and *Bitcoin Satoshi's Vision* (BSV).

Summary

Bitcoin is a profound engineering breakthrough that offers a new alternative to the existing financial system.

Bitcoin is digital money that is easy to transact worldwide given that it settles in minutes instead of days.

Bitcoin is a scarce asset, protecting against the threat of arbitrary inflation.

Bitcoin is decentralized, preventing anyone from censoring payments.

Bitcoin is the world's only decentralized, digitally scarce money.

Bitcoin has the potential to upend the current monetary order.

WHAT IS BITCOIN?

CHAPTER THREE
Bitcoin's Price and Volatility

Disclaimer: The authors of this book are not investment professionals. This chapter proposes possible reasons for bitcoin's price movement and overall volatility, and does not contain investment advice.

Everyone wants to know: Why is bitcoin valuable? Why has the price increased so much? Why is it so volatile? Why is bitcoin worth anything, if, unlike the US dollar, bitcoin isn't underwritten by an economy, or more cynically, by threats of fines and jail time?

The price of an asset moves when there is an imbalance between buyers and sellers. For bitcoin, those imbalances are driven by a few factors that differ on long-term, medium-term, and short-term perspectives.

The Long-Term Perspective

Over the past decade, the price of bitcoin has increased from a fraction of a cent to a high of nearly $20,000. The price as of August 2019 is nearly $11,000.

The Bitcoin Price from Inception to Present (Logarithmic Scale)

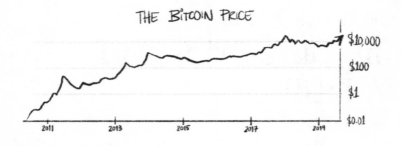

Bitcoin is scarce. The supply is set to 21 million coins as explained in Chapter 2.

Bitcoin's fixed supply and transparent issuance schedule is attractive to buyers because the alternative – fiat money – is universally subject to dilution, and thereby inflation, meaning that the same amount of money buys less every year. In the long-term, it's likely that more people will find bitcoin attractive because governments can't print more of it or censor transactions, and because it is hard to confiscate.

The total value of all bitcoin mined is still only $200 billion. By contrast, the value of all gold mined is estimated at around $9 trillion. At only 2% of the value of gold, bitcoin's market is small, and thus, more sensitive to price fluctuations. The daily volume traded is also relatively small: roughly $10 billion per day compared with $300 billion per day for gold. Because there is less *liquidity*, which is the amount that is easily bought or sold in a given period, even small buyers or sellers can have a large impact on the price. As Bitcoin adoption increases and Bitcoin grows as a global asset class, its volatility will decrease. This could take several decades.

The Medium-Term Perspective

Looking at Bitcoin in the time frame of months and years, the largest drivers of price change are mining costs, demand from large institutional buyers, and halving events.

Mining has costs: equipment, data center operations, electricity. These costs must be paid using fiat currency. Therefore, most miners will regularly sell some or all of the bitcoin they mine to pay operational costs, which roughly amount to $250-300 million per month, or 40-50% of the value of monthly mined bitcoin at the time of this writing.

Demand for bitcoin on this scale typically comes from institutional buyers, wealthy individuals, family offices, and endowments who want exposure to cryptocurrency, and typically start with bitcoin.

Another important factor influencing price in the medium-term is the *halving*. As described in Chapter 2, the mining reward reduces by half once every four years. Bitcoin has had two halvings so far, in 2012 and 2016. Both halvings created a supply cliff that spiked volatility.

Escalating bitcoin prices tend to attract more speculators, ranging from retail investors looking to buy just $100 worth of bitcoin to institutional investors buying millions of dollars worth. This, in turn, drives up the bitcoin price as media attention and the fear of missing out adds fuel to the fire. This dynamic has created large price bubbles terminating in price crashes of 80% or more. It's quite possible these price cycles will continue around future halvings.

The Short-Term Perspective

Having no central authority has an important side effect: volatility.

Where bitcoin is traded offers crucial context to the causes of short-term volatility. There are many places to do this, such as *fiat-to-crypto exchanges*, which allow trading of fiat directly to bitcoins, *peer-to-peer exchanges*, which require meeting in person, and *crypto-to-crypto exchanges*, which only allow exchanges between cryptocurrencies. Because traders seek profit from volatility, there are *leveraged exchanges*, where trading up to 100 times the deposit amount is possible.

Cryptocurrency exchanges exist primarily on the internet. They therefore operate every minute of the year, and can directly serve retail investors. By contrast, traditional markets are typically anchored in a large financial center like London, New York, or Hong Kong, are open for live trading for only about 7.5 hours Monday-Friday, and are used primarily by brokers, not retail investors.

Because anyone can send and receive bitcoin with a computer and an internet connection, it is relatively easy for an entrepreneur to set up a basic exchange. Since bitcoin is not considered a security, the exchanges on which it is traded can be subject to less stringent regulatory standards than traditional markets. Furthermore, crypto-to-crypto exchanges can shop for friendly host jurisdictions such as Malta, the Seychelles, or the Philippines, since they don't need fiat bank accounts, and teams can operate remotely. Depositing to an exchange means trusting that exchange to keep funds safe. Unfortunately, many exchanges are poorly managed. Well-documented events of malfeasance or incompetence resulting in large scale theft include Mt. Gox, Bitfinex, and Quadriga, which together lost tens of thousands of bitcoins (billions of dollars worth).

Warning to readers: a number of exchanges have been hacked or have lost their customers' bitcoins. Readers should exercise caution when using an exchange and should only risk amounts of bitcoin they're comfortable losing.

Bitcoin's suitability for retail online trading contributes to its short-term volatility. Whereas central banks usually seek to minimize volatility, traders prefer volatility because it is profitable.

Within time frames from a month down to a minute, the price volatility of bitcoin can be extreme. On January 1, 2019, one bitcoin cost $3,500. As of August 2019, it cost nearly $11,000. Daily fluctuations of up to 20% are not abnormal. This is terrifying to investors, but a paradise for speculators looking to profit from the price movement.

Unlike traditional equity or debt markets, bitcoin has no business fundamentals that determine price consensus. Bitcoin has no employees, no product performance, and no cash flows. The lack of such near-term performance indicators means an emphasis on technical elements of trading, which is often zero-sum. For such speculators, trading cryptocurrency is another form of online poker, requiring minor edges over long periods of time, played in the comfort of their living rooms and at their convenience.

As with traditional markets, bitcoin's price responds to significant news — but it doesn't always move up with good news or down with bad news. For example, in 2013, hackers attacked an exchange named Mt.Gox, the largest exchange at the time, and a significant price decline followed. However, in 2018, Binance, today's largest exchange, was hacked for about $40M and the price of bitcoin actually increased.

As bitcoin becomes more valuable and more liquid, volatility will likely be diminished. This is similar to price fluctuations in famous stocks versus lesser-known stocks. For example, it is much harder for an individual trader to move the price of Apple than the price of a penny stock.

Bitcoin is a unique and very risky vehicle for traders. The attractiveness of bitcoin to traders, combined with its lack of liquidity and the availability of leveraged trading add significant short-term volatility to its price.

Summary

Since inception, the price of bitcoin has moved up and to the right as a function of its fixed supply and increasing demand. In the near-term, the price is subject to speculation, market manipulation, and massive volatility.

Ultimately, the fixed supply and decentralized nature of Bitcoin are what give it both its value and its volatility.

If bitcoin evolves beyond a store of value and comes to represent the size of the digital economy (as fiat currency does for physical economies today), bitcoin will become a method of payment and a unit of account. At that point, volatility may decrease as bitcoin is anchored on value exchange rather than speculative activity. In the meantime, it will remain at the whim of market forces described in the <u>Medium Term</u> and <u>Short Term</u> sections in this chapter and continue to fluctuate dramatically.

CHAPTER FOUR
Why Bitcoin Matters for Human Rights

With the invention of Bitcoin, individuals are now able to consolidate the output of their hard work and store their wealth as digital information. This helps prevent regimes or corporations from arbitrarily being able to control how citizens save or transfer their money. The human rights ramifications of this financial revolution are already being felt and will continue to intensify around the world, especially in dictatorships but even in liberal democracies.

Chapter 1 introduced stories of individuals from Nigeria to Venezuela who have struggled with high inflation, financial surveillance, inaccessible banking, and broken economic infrastructures.

These are not isolated stories. According to data from the Human Rights Foundation, approximately half of the world's population lives under authoritarianism. That's approximately 4 billion people from Cuba to Belarus to Saudi Arabia to Vietnam who are severely oppressed by their governments. Many of them are economic refugees or political prisoners. These individuals don't enjoy the rule of law or the ability to push peacefully for reform. Even American and European governments financially oppress their citizens at times through ever-increasing surveillance and inflation. Banker bailouts, external military interventions, enhanced border security, and subsidized welfare are just some of the questionable activities enabled by printing more money.

When citizens are forced to use centralized payment platforms like China's WeChat which microtracks millions of lives, when a human rights group's bank account is frozen by a dictator, or when sanctions on a country punishes people for crimes their unelected rulers have committed, Bitcoin can be a way out.

Satoshi's invention can greatly help the hundreds of millions of people without bank accounts or formal identity documents to own and use money. With just a phone and internet connection, the most vulnerable individuals on the planet can receive bitcoin from anyone quickly and cheaply with no possibility of censorship or seizure.

As a result, Bitcoin is changing the game for cross-border payments and remittances, and has the potential to improve many other aspects of society. Bitcoin creates a truly global market for goods and services and can pave the way for a more level playing field.

Being Your Own Bank

In places like Bahrain, Russia, and Zimbabwe, the government exerts dictatorial control over the banking system, resulting in high levels of embezzlement and corruption. Bitcoin lays the groundwork for a world where regimes and corporations have less control and where individuals have more freedom and individual choice.

Bitcoin is a bearer instrument, meaning people can be in complete control over the bitcoin they own. Additionally, when Bitcoin is sent, there is no intermediary that can censor the transaction or leak the sender's personal information. This provides protection against thieves, malicious companies, and spying governments. No other currency or payment company can boast this kind of security.

Hiding cash under a mattress has long been a way for those in broken economies to store their money. The obvious downside is that cash is hard to secure and not convenient to transmit. If authorities show up at the front door, they can physically seize any cash they find. In comparison, bitcoin is easy to store and secure, as the private key or secret password can be stored on paper, a computer, a USB stick, or even memorized. Plausible deniability of bitcoin ownership is possible and authorities have no easy way to physically seize bitcoin.

Escaping High Inflation

Citizens of Iran to Somaliland live under regimes that recklessly print currency, draining the hard-earned savings of their economies.

Of course, inflation is something all central banks engage in. They generally consider small injections of cash into the economy desirable, as that keeps the markets in motion. Democracies may show some restraint, but as we've seen, inflation can quickly get out of control.

According to consumer price indices, from 2018 to 2019 prices rose 1.7% in Germany and 1.9% in the United States. In many countries, consumer goods prices rose much more: 3.75% in Brazil, 5% in India, 11% in Nigeria, 20% in Turkey, and a whopping 47% in Argentina. People in countries with price increases greater than 10% notice an abrupt depreciation of their earnings and savings.

An extreme case is Venezuela. Because of relentless money printing, systematic corruption, and general economic mismanagement, prices rose 2,300,000% in 2018 – a hyperinflation so severe it makes saving impossible. Money starts evaporating hours after it arrives in bank accounts. This forces Venezuelans to live hand-to-mouth, putting the money into essential goods literally as soon as they earn it. Venezuelans live under an authoritarian regime, and are unable to participate in free and fair elections by which they might hold their government accountable. In the past few years, more than 4 million citizens, who account for more than 10% of the country's population, have fled to neighboring countries, like Brazil and Colombia, in what has become one of the world's most dire refugee crises.

Besides eviscerating the domestic economy, the Venezuelan regime has imposed severe capital controls for almost two decades. Sending money into or out of the country is exceedingly difficult. The main way to send money is through intermediaries with access to accounts in two countries: an individual might give Colombian pesos to an intermediary with an account in Venezuela, who transfers the equivalent amount of Venezuelan bolivars to the final destination. Even this workaround is now being stopped as banks, under government pressure, are flagging people who use their Venezuelan accounts from abroad. Think back to Chapter 1: the regime doesn't want its population to be able to access better, sounder money than the bolivar.

Another option is to have friends or family living in the US send USD to a Western Union office in a border city in Colombia. The recipient has to escape Venezuela, travel to the city at great risk, withdraw the USD from the Western Union, and sneak back into Venezuela with cash hidden in their clothing. This is, needless to say, time-consuming and dangerous as land borders and airports are awash in corrupt officials seeking to confiscate cash.

The solution: use bitcoin to transfer value across borders. Venezuelans can ask for bitcoin from friends or family abroad via text message and receive it moments later for a small fee. This transaction isn't possible to censor and is not easy to trace.

To people living in stable economies, bitcoin may look volatile, but to Venezuelans, even an abrupt 20% fluctuation in the price of bitcoin is mild compared to the recent 2,300,000% depreciation in the bolivar.

Once they've received the bitcoin on their phone or computer, they can easily turn it into local currency through LocalBitcoins.com, an eBay-style website that connects traders in more than 100 countries. They can post the freshly-received Bitcoin for sale on the site, and get offers to buy almost immediately. Within 15 minutes they can sell the bitcoin and receive bolivares in their bank accounts. This system is used to move millions of dollars in and out of Venezuela every single day. As of mid-2019, Bitcoin has already become a parallel economy of last resort for people in completely broken economic systems like Venezuela.

Universal Access to Money

It is easy for an educated citizen of a stable democracy to open a bank account. But that's not the case for billions of people around the world. Some examples are striking. In Afghanistan and Saudi Arabia, women are prevented from opening their own bank accounts by male relatives. They are effectively stripped of their financial freedom.

For them, bitcoin can provide a lifeline. In 2014, an Afghan technology entrepreneur named Roya Mahboob faced a major challenge: she couldn't pay her female employees. If she gave them cash, their families would take it away. Male relatives would not let them open bank accounts. Software like PayPal wasn't available in their country. A friend mentioned the possibility of using bitcoin and she started using it to pay her employees. It gave them financial self-sovereignty.

One of these young women had to flee Afghanistan because of a threat on her life. But she took her bitcoin with her, stored on her phone. She traveled through Iran and Turkey and eventually made it to Germany. There, she exchanged her bitcoin — which thankfully had appreciated dramatically during her journey — into euros to start a new life. Bitcoin can help the oppressed and unbanked when there are no other options.

As Bitcoin's infrastructure and local person-to-person exchanges grow in the coming years, it will have a major impact on foreign aid and humanitarian assistance. Perhaps the most vivid picture of what's wrong in the aid industry is a photo that came out of the Venezuelan border in February 2019, when the Maduro regime prevented foreign aid from coming into the country by barricading the border bridge with tractor-trailers. Not visible in the photo were the millions of dollars in bitcoin moving back and forth beyond government control.

Today's foreign-aid system has glaring vulnerabilities. Whether it is a government sending aid to another government, a philanthropic organization making a gift to an NGO, or an individual sending money to family in a medical emergency, money only arrives at its destination after traveling through third parties.

Even in the most basic situation, there are at least three inter-mediaries: the sender's bank, a central bank, and the receiver's bank. There are often more intermediaries, sometimes as many as seven. Each can slow the process, freeze the transaction, or even steal the money. Former U.N. Secretary-General Ban Ki-moon declared in a 2012 speech that during the previous year corruption had "prevented 30% of all development assistance from reaching its final destination."

According to research by organizations like GiveDirectly and the World Bank, direct cash transfers are the most effective way to deliver aid. Bitcoin enables permissionless transfers to anyone on the planet within minutes. The recipient doesn't need a bank account or official identification, just internet access.

A recent study by Pew found that 45% of people in emerging economies already own a smartphone, a number that continues to rise. To understand the potential impact of Bitcoin in this area, consider that in a country like the Philippines, only 20% of adults have a bank account.

To be used as a payment rail, bitcoin recipients must be able to trade it into local currency. Bitcoin is not currently useful as aid unless it can be spent for goods or services. But according to a detailed analysis of bitcoin marketplace data carried out by Matt Ahlborg, it is becoming easier for individuals in emerging economies from East Asia to West Africa to exchange bitcoin into local currencies.

What's more, when traditional banks shut down, the Bitcoin network keeps going. As its worldwide infrastructure improves liquidity and access for people around the world, Bitcoin's ability to act as a lifeline for those receiving aid will increase dramatically.

There already exist mesh networks, satellite systems, and radio-based techniques which allow people to send and receive bitcoin without access to the internet. Engineers are working on innovations to make it harder and harder for governments to prevent citizens from accessing bitcoin, a currency that they cannot inflate or easily confiscate.

The Cashless Society

The idea of a cashless society is often presented as very convenient. But from the human rights perspective, it presents new dangers while giving governments and banks unprecedented power.

Cash is one of the best ways to protect a person's privacy. When paying for something with a paper note, only the buyer and the seller know about the transaction, and purchasing behavior becomes difficult for governments to track. Anonymous payments are possible with cash as when paper notes are dropped into a charity donations box.

Unfortunately, cash is disappearing around the world. In hyperinflated societies such as Venezuela or Somaliland, paper notes are so worthless that they need to be weighed in bunches by the kilo. Meanwhile, in advanced urban areas such as Stockholm and Shanghai, residents employ digital payments almost exclusively. It's estimated that only 8% of all global transactions are still carried out with coins or notes. By 2030, the number of people who can meaningfully use cash in their daily lives will be close to zero.

As seen in Chapter 1, this can be a scary prospect for protestors who rely on cash in places like Hong Kong to buy public transit tickets or burner SIM cards to protect privacy and fight surveillance. Without cash, or some digital equivalent, coordinating political protests while protecting personal safety will become almost impossible.

In Estonia, the government is making public transportation free. It sounds wonderful but comes with a catch: passengers can only get free rides by using their citizen cards, thus enabling the government to track their movements. While Estonians may not have to worry, citizens of nearby authoritarian governments such as Russia or Belarus have serious reason to be concerned.

Meanwhile the Chinese Communist Party has control over systems with more than a billion users like Alipay or WeChat. Authorities don't just exert surveillance and control over people's money, they also regulate their citizens' actions and opinions through social credit systems. In social credit systems, such as the one being implemented across China, citizens are scored not just on their financial health but also on their political opinions, identity, and social circle. The government incentivizes loyal citizen behavior and punishes troublemakers by preventing them from traveling abroad, getting fast internet, sending their kids to good schools, or getting good rates on loans. These social credit systems are still nascent, but are on track to give unprecedented control to the Chinese government and constitute the largest social engineering project in human history.

Similar, though less distressing trends are beginning to emerge even in Western democracies, with credit card companies and merchants selling transaction activity to advertisers for profit.

Bitcoin vs. Big Brother

What people buy reveals more than what they say. Transactions disclose a huge amount about who people are and what they do, where they go and when, or what they like or dislike.

The more extensively spending is tracked, the more likely individuals are to face an Orwellian outcome.

In democratic societies, there is a debate emerging with regard to the role of corporations like Facebook as issuers of their own currencies. Facebook is proposing to introduce Libra to hundreds of millions of people via existing social media accounts on WhatsApp, Instagram, or Messenger. While a project like Libra could very well grant financial access to large numbers of people who are currently unbanked, many fear Facebook will record the payment activity of users, influence choices, or deplatform individuals and freeze their ability to make payments for expressing particular political opinions.

To stop Big Brother, everyone must reduce their ever-expanding data footprints. The less that identity-linked information is disseminated and shared between companies and governments, the harder individuals are to surveil, manipulate, and control.

A cashless society is a surveillance society. Whether it is with the government-controlled WeChat model or the corporate-controlled Libra model, companies can track all economic activity for profit, oppression or worse.

What if the future could be different? What if cash could exist in a digital form? Although currently bitcoin transactions are only pseudonymous, there is much work being done in the developer community to bring more privacy to the Bitcoin network and its users. In the near future, when buying something online, purchasing a bus or subway ticket, or subscribing to political magazines or podcasts, individuals won't need to disclose their identity when making payments.

Making Bitcoin Private with the Lightning Network

Consumers are increasingly losing financial privacy. A solution may exist with Lightning, a payment network currently being built on top of Bitcoin.

The existing payment system creates all sorts of privacy honeypots, as every financial intermediary is a potential security hole. Bitcoin is different in that there are no intermediaries, so that at least in principle, this vulnerability could be eliminated. Key details of bitcoin transactions are unfortunately recorded in the blockchain, which anyone can see. Researchers have explored whether there is a way to hide or obscure the specific details of a transaction and still pay with bitcoin, and this is possible with Lightning.

The Lightning Network doesn't record the details of each transaction to the Bitcoin blockchain directly. The goal of Lightning is to increase the speed and volume of transactions Bitcoin can handle. Privacy happens to be a side effect of achieving that goal.

This technical breakthrough is much like Bitcoin in that it is open-source, permissionless, and available to anyone, regardless of location, age, income, gender, or citizenship. Bitcoin on Lightning could help prevent a dystopian future in which privacy is expensive and only attainable by wealthy individuals.

Even in a cashless society, it should soon be possible to use a Lightning app on a phone to anonymously buy transit tickets to attend a demonstration or purchase political books online. The metro ticket machine or Amazon won't know anything about the purchasers, and won't be able to leak their data or share their information with governments.

That said, Lightning is not a privacy panacea. Anonymizing payment information is only one step towards securing full privacy, as privacy gaps like backdoors on phones, geolocation tracking, and surveillance cameras also need to be abolished.

Black Swan author Nassim Taleb has written that Bitcoin is "an insurance policy against an Orwellian future." As worldwide trends of growing surveillance and disappearing cash continue, that future seems to be pressing on us.

Technology doesn't always improve freedom around the world. On the contrary, artificial intelligence and big data analysis are systematically stripping individuals of their liberties, especially in places like China. The historian and *Sapiens* author Yuval Noah Harari has warned that modern information technology tends to favor tyranny, but technology can also favor freedom when designed and deployed deliberately with this purpose. Bitcoin, especially when it is empowered with new developments like the Lightning Network, can be an important tool in the global struggle for human rights.

CHAPTER FIVE
A Tale of Two Futures

The year is 2039.

The past 20 years have seen a significant rise in global war. Countries fight to unseat the US dollar and Chinese renminbi from their dominant positions. Sometimes this economic turbulence breaks out into violent conflict. Rich countries suffer from political decline and intractable economic recession, while poor countries hover near total collapse as successive economic crises consolidate wealth and power to central state and corporate powers.

Dominant tech companies such as Alibaba, Tencent, Facebook, Google, and Amazon control the global marketplace, and after several rounds of government pressure, antitrust lawsuits, and settlements, they've agreed to hand over user data in exchange for market protection. Companies share comprehensive user information with governments around the world about what everyone buys, what everyone listens to, what everyone is posting about, and where everyone is. Companies have become satellites of the state. Personal privacy is nonexistent.

This gives governments unprecedented control over their citizens. The gap between the rich and the poor continues to widen, as the Cantillon Effect magnifies and those with regime connections prosper in a disproportionate way. Digital surveillance is the norm while criticism of authoritarian governments evaporates. Government and corporate control of money means they can censor speech, as dissenting content creators cannot get paid or supported to do their work.

Diversity of thought is now dissent. Police states around the world use the internet of things, medical implant data, phone tracking, transaction histories, and search queries to locate and punish dissidents. Opposition is essentially impossible, as cash has disappeared and all purchases (including for items like metro tickets, newspapers, and masks that could conceal one's identity) are digital and monitored. The state and multinational corporations are more powerful than ever.

The year is 2039.

A vibrant global economy continues to flourish. More people around the world are saving, accumulating wealth, able to afford homes, and running new businesses. Entrepreneurs from what used to be called third-world countries are driving innovation in the global economy. Moving jurisdictions is easier than ever. Governments compete as citizens choose where they want to live, work, and pay taxes. Income taxes decrease, while the quality of infrastructure, services, and schools all increase as a result of global competition.

The proliferation of so many new goods and services provided by so many more small enterprises has brought forth more innovation than thought possible. Many multinational corporations that used to dominate the marketplace have been out-classed by the numerous smaller players from all corners of the globe. Anyone can pay for anything using permissionless and private payments.

Many authoritarian regimes have been toppled or weakened as citizens become more adept at skirting draconian capital controls and preserving wealth for themselves instead of ceding it to the elites.

Governments have been forced to move from controlling to competing; individuals are freer than ever before.

What Does a More Bitcoin-based World Look Like?

Predicting the future is always a risky proposition. These are two alternate visions given the world's current trajectory. Neither extreme is likely to materialize, but individuals have control over what direction their society will take.

The monetary system sits in the middle of the crossroads. Bitcoin has the potential to separate money and state. It is worth asking, how could global Bitcoin adoption change society?

The Borderless Economy Emerges

Since the 20th century, economies have largely been controlled by nation-states. The transition to digital money initially allowed governments to control economies in an unprecedented way by easily increasing the money supply to pay for initiatives.

But as the digital era advanced, economies started to transcend states. At the beginning of the 21st century, this was obvious as consumers bought goods produced halfway around the world. Companies hired freelancers from the Philippines to Nigeria as software developers, virtual assistants, or even remote radiologists. Trading partners could be separated by thousands of miles. All communication was digital, instant, and seamless. Making cross-border payments however, was still slow and expensive. Paying for online goods still relied on traditional channels, and settlement in USD between financial institutions still took several days. The money system hadn't yet adapted to match the increasingly connected world.

The emergence of Bitcoin is the spark that will enable the next wave of financial evolution.

Digitally-native goods such as social media content and video game items will consume a larger share of the world economy. Bitcoin will increasingly be used as a method of payment in cross-border transactions because fiat will remain cumbersome. Bitcoin's microtransactions, fast settlement, and growing user base will compel merchants to denominate prices in bitcoin.

These economies are small today — like communities chatting on AOL in the 1990s — but as they grow, they will further erode the economic control of states. As more wealth is sourced from borderless networks and denominated in a borderless currency owned by individuals, wealth will become easier to move and will become liberated from the physical economy of any single nation-state.

Governments Face the True Price of War

When bitcoin becomes ubiquitous, the ability of the state to simply print more money to fund war will be much more limited. Wars will no longer be financed as easily as they have been over the past hundred years. If wars do happen, they will be more limited and briefer.

Prolonged conflicts like the Russian intervention of Syria and Ukraine or the American occupation of Iraq and Afghanistan may become a thing of the past, as such operations will become increasingly difficult to finance. War between nation-states becomes even more of a last ditch option than it is today, as governments are much more incentivized to find less expensive ways to settle disagreements.

Authoritarianism Becomes Too Expensive

Authoritarian states will have a difficult time competing in a global environment that's harder for them to control. With individuals across the world controlling their personal value transfer, the most productive citizens of any country will simply leave *with their wealth* to a competing jurisdiction if conditions are undesirable. To keep those productive citizens, governments will have to enforce severe border controls or give such citizens a voice in their own governance.

Dictatorships aren't going to go away quietly, but they will be forced into a choice: face mass capital flight or allow more freedom. Thanks to information networks, liberal works of literature and film now routinely make their way into households living under even the most tyrannical regimes like Eritrea and North Korea. This phenomenon will be accelerated by money that is as transferable and securable as information.

Assets Become Correctly Priced

Bitcoin provides a store of value for everyone, regardless of status or ethnicity or geographic location. As a reaction to fiat money inflation, most people currently choose to store some of their wealth in real estate, stocks, and precious metals, all of which are more centralized and therefore harder to access than bitcoin. In a world where storage of wealth in Bitcoin is the norm, speculative bubbles in these assets will no longer be as prevalent.

For example, there will be fewer cases of inflation-induced housing bubbles, as fewer foreigners will buy large chunks of a city's housing supply with no plans to live there. With bitcoin as a superior alternative, buying stable assets abroad won't be attractive. Prices won't skyrocket and more people will be able to afford homes in their own cities.

Decentralized Finance Arrives

American, European, and Chinese domination will fade as countries are able to settle trades in bitcoin, a true global reserve currency, instead of the regional USD, EUR, or CNY. Workforces will be free to move about the world and there will be more competition for labor, giving workers more of the value they produce.

US, European, and Chinese banks will lose their oppressive influence, since each person can be their own bank, allowing true savings over time. Wealth will accumulate in countries that export labor, allowing domestic businesses to spring up and infrastructure and services to be built.

The Power of Big Banks Shrinks

Banks, which have grown huge because of their special relationship with governments and their control over people's money, will either go bankrupt or become much smaller. "Too big to fail" will no longer be the norm, and banks and larger corporations will no longer be able to depend on government bailouts whenever they make mistakes, as in the 2008 financial crisis.

Without these advantages, banks and multinational corporations will need to focus on providing services to their customers, rather than pandering to governments for handouts. Smaller companies and banks, thanks to the borderless nature of bitcoin, will be able to serve customers worldwide and will displace the ossified giants of the past.

Decline of Big Brother and Surveillance Capitalism

Today, digital payment information is both exploited by companies for profit and used for government surveillance. Because the internet evolved as a default open marketplace, privacy standards have been slow to protect the increasingly personal and important information that is online. As a result, personal data is constantly repackaged, analyzed, and used without knowledge or explicit permission.

With the advent and adoption of the Lightning payments on top of Bitcoin, most small daily purchases will be disconnected from identity.

When buying something online, subscribing to a political magazine, donating to a civil society organization, or paying for a medical treatment, no one other than the consumer will know the full details of the transaction. There will be no payment processor to leak information from an intermediary position, as the transactions are peer to peer with the merchant seeing only the payment. With no identifying information in this environment, it will be much harder for surveillance systems to track consumers' behavior and predict their actions.

The Start of Self-Sovereignty

Bitcoin is a phenomenon similar in potential impact to democracy and the internet: technologies which respectively overthrew the tyranny of political power and corporate control of knowledge. Through democracy, citizens collectively keep the power of government and dictators in check, and through the internet, average citizens gain a stronger voice and freer access to knowledge.

Along the same lines, Bitcoin will shatter the monetary monopoly enjoyed by states and corporations. A century from now, individuals will look back at 2019 and remember a time when the privileged few controlled the economy as outdated, just like someone today looks back on the idea of the monarchical feudal system or state propaganda as outdated. This evolution will take place in three phases as bitcoin evolves into the currency of the world.

Phase 1: Store of Value

The first step of Bitcoin adoption will be as a store of value. This is the stage in which savers all over the world protect themselves against the inflation of their local governments. This is happening today not just in hyperinflated economies like those of Venezuela and Zimbabwe, but also in places like the United States and Europe where bitcoin has, over multi-year stretches, outperformed the local fiat currency. Late in the Store of Value phase, pension funds and mainstream financial institutions will start adding bitcoin to their portfolios, and still later, governments will start to add bitcoin to their reserves.

Adoption during this phase will grow slowly and organically as people realize its benefits.

Phase 2: Method of Payment

When enough merchants realize that non-bitcoin money is in fact an inferior store of value, they'll want to be paid in bitcoin. This is akin to black-market merchants in Venezuela who refuse bolivars and demand US dollars. As more merchants, entrepreneurs, and employees come to prefer bitcoin, the demand for bitcoin will rise in the same way that the demand for US dollars skyrocketed following the introduction of the Bretton Woods gold convertibility system.

This won't happen initially in advanced economies like that of the United States, but instead in broken economies with wild inflation and intractable corruption. These societies will likely be ruled by oppressive regimes that diminish the usefulness of easily confiscated stores of value like USD notes and gold. People in such places will use bitcoin to evade seizure of their wealth, and if necessary, to escape entirely.

In this phase, well-designed software, quicker settlement technologies, improved infrastructure, and privacy innovations will come to the forefront. Bitcoin users will be able to conduct transactions instantly and privately, making surveillance much harder.

Phase 3: Unit of Account

As more people hold and earn bitcoin instead of their local currency, goods and services will start being priced in their absolute bitcoin price instead of the local currency or the USD. At this point, there will be lucrative arbitrage opportunities, whereby taking out loans in rapidly depreciating currencies and converting them to bitcoin will become profitable.

This will be the beginning of hyperbitcoinization, where the USD and CNY will lose their privileged positions and bitcoin will become the world settlement currency. This, in turn, will cause hyperinflation on the part of most other currencies as loans will be very expensive to prevent arbitrage. As Bitcoin will be the most desirable place to store value, the positive feedback loop will cause many other currencies to depreciate substantially.

It Is Still Early

Most world-changing technologies are dismissed by the crowd at first. Consider electricity, which was considered very dangerous; the telephone, which no one wanted to buy; the car, which surely couldn't work on cobblestone roads; the plane, which couldn't possibly be safe; the microwave, which supposedly removed all nutritional value from food; the mobile phone, which allegedly caused cancer; or the internet, which was destined to fail. Remember the words of the *New York Times* columnist Paul Krugman, who wrote in 1998 that "by 2005, it will become clear that the Internet's impact on the economy has been no greater than the fax machine."

Any fundamental technology, from the refrigerator to the credit card, follows an adoption curve, and there are always plenty of skeptics at the beginning. Eventually, the curve rises exponentially, making the shape of an S, and the technology spreads. It is hard to imagine a more fair or democratic idea than the fact that anyone today — regardless of their location, gender, language, age, level of education, or wealth — can get meaningfully involved with Bitcoin, an exponential technology that is still at the bottom of its adoption S-curve.

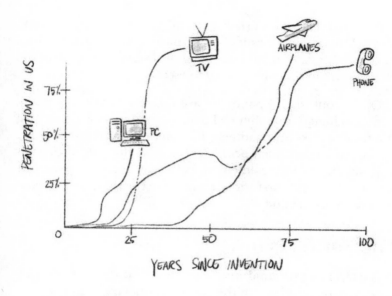

Bitcoin is currently far from where it needs to be in terms of usability, capacity, public awareness, and commercial interest. There aren't enough companies building on Bitcoin; not enough students focusing on it; not enough teachers assigning it; not enough merchants accepting it; not enough philanthropic foundations supporting its development; and not enough public leaders taking its ability to help achieve financial privacy seriously. More interest, engagement, and critical thinking is needed in this area.

Less than 1% of the world's population has ever owned bitcoin. If the proper time and resources are invested in developing user-friendly wallets, exchanges, and educational materials, Bitcoin has the potential to make a real difference for billions around the world. Bitcoin can help anyone achieve more financial freedom, but it will likely first help those who need it the most.

People in Nigeria, Turkey, the Philippines, Venezuela, Iran, China, Russia, or Palestine don't have the same freedoms, human rights, and trust in their financial system as those in the West. For them, Bitcoin is a way to escape.

Opting out, silence, and exit are the new forms of protest. To enact change, an individual doesn't need to coordinate with thousands of like-minded people to flood the streets for a day or week at a time. Such people can export their wealth just as easily as they can send an email. Protests can now happen one person at a time. At first adoption will be a trickle, then a stream, and eventually a flood.

The Future Is in Your Hands

Bitcoin is a profound invention that provides new alternatives to many problems of the current monetary and economic system. Inequality, monopolistic multinational corporations, and authoritarianism are, in part, fueled by the state control of money. As the world learns about Bitcoin and how it enables self-sovereignty, power will decentralize in significant ways all over the world. Instead of authoritarian regimes, governments will be forced to trend towards respecting human dignity, value, and talent. Instead of disconnected multinational corporations, there will be smaller companies that work to serve their customers. While equality of outcome is not possible, Bitcoin will level the playing field by enabling humans to capture and hold on to the value they create.

What could be more fair than the idea that all that is needed to participate in the next financial revolution is access to an inexpensive smartphone and to the internet? No bank, no government regulator, no permission is required to be a part of this future.

By taking back control of wealth from the whims of those in control, everyone can be freer to create their own destiny.

Bitcoin enables human freedom in a way never thought possible at the start of the 21st century.

Pass this book on and help spread the word.

Bitcoin Q&A

Over the past few years, newcomers and skeptics have asked a lot of questions about Bitcoin. This section tries to answer the important and frequent ones, addressing some of the myths, challenges, downsides, and common confusions around Bitcoin. This section aims to provide enough fundamental information to get a curious mind off to a strong start but isn't by any means exhaustive.

Who is Satoshi Nakamoto?

Satoshi Nakamoto is the anonymous creator of Bitcoin.

In the first two years of Bitcoin's history, Satoshi Nakamoto was an active member of the community. Satoshi posted online frequently with thoughts on Bitcoin's technology and its social impact while contributing to software development. In late 2010, Satoshi disappeared.

Satoshi likely owns hundreds of millions of dollars worth of bitcoin, which anyone can see on the blockchain. These coins have never moved, suggesting the disappearance might be permanent. As of this writing, Satoshi's identity has not been revealed, making this one of the greatest mysteries of the 21st century.

Who controls Bitcoin?

There is no central authority in charge of Bitcoin. There is no CEO, no board of directors, and no controlling company. One of Bitcoin's strongest attributes is that its creator is no longer involved.

There are thousands of validators around the world who verify Bitcoin's blockchain, and store the complete history of bitcoin transactions. These validators are called *full nodes*.

As discussed in Chapter 2, miners around the world compete to produce blocks. Those blocks are validated by the full nodes. The software used to run those full nodes are written by Bitcoin developers. And of course the transactions within those blocks are initiated by users from their exchanges, wallets, or payment processors. All of these participants are essential for Bitcoin to function, but none of them *control* Bitcoin.

If a developer decides to create full node software that is radically different, few will run that software. If a miner tries to sneak in a new block of transactions that don't meet the validation requirements, the full nodes will reject that block. If miners attempt a coup d'état to impose new features on the network, they will fail as they cannot force users to run software that they don't want to run.

Thus, any change in Bitcoin requires consensus. In this sense, the Bitcoin governance model is similar to a democracy with checks and balances. The miners are like the executive branch of government, handling operations and enforcing the rules; developers are like the legislative branch, developing and passing new laws; users are the judicial branch, making sure the other two branches don't do anything unconstitutional.

Isn't Bitcoin too volatile?

Bitcoin has experienced tremendous volatility since its creation in 2009. Viewed over a longer time frame, Bitcoin has appreciated significantly since inception, from less than $.001 to more than $11,000 at the time of this writing. As explained in Chapter 3, several factors have driven its price up over the long term and likely will continue to do so.

Satoshi Nakamoto set Bitcoin's monetary policy at inception. No single person or group can decide to create more bitcoin or change its supply schedule as full nodes will reject such a change.

As a result, Bitcoin will be more vulnerable to market manipulation since it has no central banking correction mechanism. A central bank can print new money or buy more of its own money back as a way to maintain price stability. As a decentralized currency, with no corrective regulators, it will continue to experience volatility as it is adopted around the world.

The economic reality is this: currencies have to choose between short-term price stability through centralization or potential for a long-term price appreciation through decentralization. Satoshi Nakamoto chose decentralization.

Most importantly, the volatility of bitcoin has not prevented it from having tremendous real-world value as a financial tool for people who are trapped in broken financial systems. Use-cases for Bitcoin include escape from sanctions, hyperinflation, capital controls, and surveillance. For now, the day-to-day volatility is a trade off owners have been willing to pay.

What actually backs Bitcoin's value?

This short answer is that people back Bitcoin. Enough investors buy it, so it has value. Refer to Chapter 3 for a detailed explanation of what gives Bitcoin its historically-rising price. There is global demand for bitcoin as an asset that is scarce, has utility, and does things as a technology that no other financial tool can do.

How can Bitcoin be trusted?

The modern world is full of complex systems or devices that aren't fully understood, yet trusted. Health care is provided to people who are not doctors. Weather forecasts are published for non-meteorologists. Laptops are used by people who are not electrical engineers. Travellers don't have to understand aerodynamics in order to travel on planes.

The standards for trusting new money systems should be more stringent, as there are frequent abuses of that trust, many which have been documented throughout this book. But ultimately, subject matter expertise will not be necessary to use and trust Bitcoin. Eventually, sending and receiving bitcoin will be as easy as sending and receiving an email. For now, those interested in Bitcoin should definitely do their own research. Many good sources of information are listed in the *Additional Resources* section of this book, including the Bitcoin Core source code, other books, websites, and podcasts.

How reliable is Bitcoin?

When used properly, Bitcoin is much safer, more robust, and more private than any centralized payment processor. Mastercard and Visa, for example, have outages from time to time. Bitcoin has been fully operational for 99.98% of its history since launching in January 2009. Credit card companies also regularly sell customer information and get hacked. Bitcoin can't sell any information about its users because there's no one in control. Unlike payment processors and many banks, Bitcoin has not been meaningfully hacked since the price rose above $0.10 in 2010. No one's coins have ever been stolen at the network level. This is a remarkable track record.

Why have so many Bitcoin exchanges been hacked?

Cryptocurrency exchanges are very popular, both as a place for investors to buy bitcoin for the first time and also as a place for speculators to trade bitcoin against fiat currency or other cryptocurrencies. As a result, exchanges hold large amounts of bitcoin and fiat on behalf of their customers, which make them attractive targets for hackers and thieves. Custodial services also store copies of personal IDs, passports and home addresses of their customers as part of their KYC ("Know Your Customer") procedures.

Attacks can occur both internally and externally. Internal attacks may come from employees who have privileged access to the exchange's system and use that to steal customer funds. External attacks are carried out by hackers who use software vulnerabilities, weak operational security, and social engineering to steal bitcoins.

Many exchanges have been attacked both internally and externally. Just a few examples include Mt.Gox in Japan, Bitfinex in Hong Kong, Bitstamp in the EU, and more recently Quadriga in Canada. Each resulted in millions of dollars in lost bitcoins. These hacks stand as a strong warning to users who allow someone else to take custody of their bitcoin. Customers who trade on exchanges can withdraw their bitcoins periodically into personal wallets to avoid any potential losses from hacks.

Do criminals use bitcoin for money laundering?

Yes. Criminals have used bitcoin for money laundering and illegal activities, and they will continue to do so. The most famous case is the Silk Road, a darknet marketplace where bitcoin was used to buy and sell drugs considered illegal in the United States.

Because Bitcoin is a permissionless technology, anyone can use it, like the mobile phone or the internet. Few question the legitimacy of these ubiquitous technologies today or call for their ban because bad actors use them. Many people direct hostile skepticism at technologies when they are first emerging.

In any case, the absolute majority of financial crime in today's world is carried out using the existing financial system via regulated banks and money transmitters. Most fraud is committed by governments and multinational corporations, not by rogue individuals. Democratic governments have put anti-money laundering rules (AML) in place to pressure banks to stop certain transactions, yet more than $1 trillion continues to be laundered through the banking system every single year. To give one example, reports recently disclosed that a single office of Danske Bank in Denmark had laundered a staggering $230 billion, which is more than the market value of all bitcoins in circulation at the time of this writing.

So although criminals have used bitcoin, criminals prefer the fiat money system.

Is Bitcoin a Ponzi scheme?

A Ponzi scheme promises investors large profits with very little risk. Ponzi schemes achieve these returns for their earliest investors by paying them with money collected from later investors. There is no real profit-making mechanism aside from trying to get as many new investors as possible to pay off those that came before. These schemes collapse when there are no new investors to be found.

Bitcoin is not a Ponzi scheme. There is no group of people behind Bitcoin trying to lure new buyers into pay off old buyers. People who orchestrate Ponzi schemes, however, can accept bitcoin from their investors in the same way they do with all other forms of money.

Is Bitcoin a bubble?

A bubble happens when speculative investors purchase a financial asset en masse at a price far beyond what is justifiable by its fundamental value. Bubbles always pop as soon as faith in the asset is lost, and no other investors are willing to buy at the asking price. Historical examples include Dutch tulips in the 1500s, the South Sea Company in the 1700s, and Dotcom stocks in the early 2000s.

Chapter 3 described some of the main drivers of Bitcoin price volatility. Owing to the natural volatility of an asset with a rigid monetary policy, regular supply shocks, the instability and collapse of other cryptocurrencies, market manipulation, and the leveraged nature of bitcoin trading, there have been several price spikes that have been followed by significant crashes. This is a trend that is likely to continue.

When considering the long-term value, price drivers, and decentralized nature of Bitcoin, its value should naturally increase as more people use it. Unlike tulips or Dotcom stocks, Bitcoin's value has repeatedly recovered and trended upward after each major market crash as more and more people around the world acquire bitcoins.

What is Tether and how does it affect Bitcoin?

Tether, or USDT is a coin that is supposed to be pegged to the US dollar. To achieve this, the company behind Tether intended to back each Tether token in circulation with one US dollar in the company's bank account. This made it easier to speculate on cryptocurrency since most people still think in fiat, so having USDT as a proxy for US dollars has made it possible for anyone on the many crypto-to-crypto exchanges to actively trade against the US dollar.

However, in April 2019, Tether's general counsel revealed that they only had US dollars to back 74% of Tethers in circulation. If Tether's dollar peg breaks, its price collapse may cause short-term bitcoin volatility — but there are a number of competitors to Tether that are well poised to fill its role.

Can governments ban or turn off Bitcoin?

Because there is no company, no centrally coordinated set of servers, and no single team running Bitcoin, there's no practical way to shut down the network.

Bitcoin is open-source software, meaning that the source code is openly available on the internet. Corrupting or changing that software is very difficult because people are watching. Anyone can download, use, copy, and run the Bitcoin software and validate the ledger. This is called running a full node. The more full nodes are on the network, the more resilient Bitcoin becomes.

Governments can make Bitcoin harder to use, but it then becomes a game of whack-a-mole. Consider the experience of trading fiat currency for Bitcoin in a country like China. As mentioned in Chapter 1, Chinese individuals are limited to converting $50,000 each year out of their CNY yet they continue to use bitcoin to move money abroad.

Even a large, wealthy, police state cannot prevent its citizenry from using Bitcoin. Because the network has no single point of failure, governments cannot turn off the Bitcoin network.

Bitcoin is similar to the internet in this way. A government can prevent citizens from accessing parts of the internet, for example, the Great Chinese Firewall, but censored citizens will use tools like VPNs and ingenuity to get around these restrictions. No government can block access to the Bitcoin network without removing access to the internet itself, a cost that few governments beyond North Korea seem willing to incur.

Authoritarian governments could ban the possession of bitcoin, but enforcement would be exceedingly difficult. Due to its digital nature, hiding bitcoin is relatively easy. Storing bitcoin on a phone, on a USB device, or even in one's mind are all options that are very difficult to discover and penalize. In contrast, gold, real estate, stocks, and fiat in bank accounts are all relatively easy for governments to locate and confiscate.

Is Bitcoin legal?

Mostly, yes. As of August 2019, its possession is permitted in all countries except Namibia, Algeria, Bolivia, Iraq, Morocco, Nepal, Pakistan, UAE, and Vietnam. From a regulatory standpoint, Bitcoin has come a long way: in the last 10 years, Bitcoin has progressed from being seen as the money of online criminals to being acknowledged by the IMF, members of the US Congress, and Wall Street.

In China, the government has policed cryptocurrency exchanges and the creation of new tokens, but bitcoin is legally recognized as digital property. Even in Iran, bitcoin mining is now a legalized industry.

On the African continent, the governments of most countries have no public stance. In places like Nigeria and Kenya, public officials warn against its use, but there are no concrete regulations. South Africa is currently the only African country where bitcoin is officially accepted and regulated.

In Canada, the US, and the EU, the possession and use of bitcoin is legal.

A few countries have created a specific licensing framework for companies that wish to operate cryptocurrency exchanges. These include Japan, Malta, the Philippines, and Thailand.

Tax implications are more complicated and are determined by the way each government classifies bitcoin. If a tax authority considers bitcoin property, then individuals will be taxed accordingly on its acquisition, liquidation, appreciation, and depreciation, similar to a piece of real estate.

Looking to the future, if governments wanted to conspire to ban bitcoin, it is unlikely that they could come to an agreement. Even if some countries succeeded in establishing a ban, other countries would step in and welcome bitcoin miners, entrepreneurs, and traders. There would be a migration of talent and wealth to those friendlier jurisdictions, making the restrictive governments rethink their policies.

Is bitcoin mining a waste of energy or bad for the environment?

As of June 2019, the Bitcoin network consumes about 73 terawatt-hours of electricity per year. This is slightly more consumption than the country of Austria (69 terawatt-hours per year), but much less than China (6,100 terawatt-hours per year) and the United States (3,900 terawatt-hours per year), the two biggest energy consumers.

Critics are quick to point out that this is an enormous amount of power. While that is technically true, it does not address whether Bitcoin wastes energy or is bad for the environment. The sources of energy that Bitcoin miners typically use and the value Bitcoin provides can provide some context.

Preventing Energy Waste with Bitcoin Mining

Bitcoin mining can help excess capacity find a good use. Mining is both a mobile and low-margin business. Therefore, mining companies have an especially large incentive and ability to physically seek out the cheapest possible electricity. Frequently, the cheapest sources of energy are in remote or inaccessible locations where there is unused capacity.

The majority of Bitcoin mining takes place in China, where power plants collectively produce a surplus of 200 terawatt-hours at any given time. Since it is not possible to store this much power (the largest battery farm in the world can only hold about 0.5% of that amount) — and since it is not possible to effectively transmit the power to remote regions — the electricity normally goes untapped. Rather than wasting that potential, power plants can purchase bitcoin mining equipment and turn the excess energy into new bitcoins. This is true in any location where an energy source generates too much for immediate use.

Bitcoin Mining's Reliance on Renewable Energy

The majority of bitcoin mining today is done with renewable energy that has a minimal cost to the environment. According to the latest estimates, about 75% of all bitcoin mining is currently done with hydroelectric, solar, wind, and geothermal sources of energy. About 50% of renewable energy bitcoin mining is done in one area of China, powered by hydroelectric dams.

Hydroelectric power plants have massive energy production capacity, but are often underutilized. Bitcoin mining puts the excess capacity to use as the mining operation can be placed next to the hydroelectric plant, eliminating transmission costs. The revenue generated makes production and research of hydroelectric power more profitable, encouraging its use. In this way, Bitcoin mining subsidizes hydroelectric power.

Mining may also incentivize more solar, wind, and geothermal energy production.

Bitcoin Mining Enables Secure, Accessible Money

Bitcoin miners provide security for the network. As discussed in chapter 2, the electricity required by miners to search for rare proof-of-work numbers in order to propose valid blocks makes fraud very costly. The more bitcoin mining there is, the harder it is to attack the network. The energy used to secure the ledger can be compared to the cost of creating and maintaining a high-security vault that protects $200 billion in assets.

Bitcoin might be just one of many financial options for those living in the first world, but in other parts of the world, payment services like Venmo or ApplePay are not available. Dismissing Bitcoin mining as a waste of energy is discounting the utility Bitcoin gives to the technological underclass. Part of this energy goes towards processing transactions for people who don't have bank accounts or IDs, or who don't want their financial activity tightly surveilled by governments. Banks and credit cards may exceed Bitcoin's utility in a place like the United States, but do nothing for an unbanked migrant worker in Dubai or an Iranian living under UN sanctions.

Energy Use and Technological Innovation

Bitcoin is a major technical innovation, enabling many things outlined in this book that the current monetary system cannot do. Historically, new technology uses more energy than old systems that they displace. For example, consider the disruption of the horse by the car; the field tent by the modern hospital; hand washing by a washing machine; an ice-box by refrigerator; and oil lamps by electric lamps. The electricity cost of the technical innovation is offset by the improved quality of life that it facilitates. As civilization advances, more energy is expended per individual. Innovation enhances society, and no innovation is adopted without some tradeoffs. The tradeoffs in Bitcoin are electricity usage in return for a fair, convenient and secure monetary system. Bitcoin uses a lot of energy, but is driving innovation for renewable energy. Bitcoin provides tremendous value, especially for the poor and oppressed, and replaces a flawed, older system that uses even more energy.

What if someone with a supercomputer or quantum computer hacks the Bitcoin network?

In theory, the Bitcoin network can be compromised by an attacker with enough computing power. In practice, that's very difficult to do.

Using current hardware, an attacker must finance, build, and operate a mining facility at a cost of more than $1 billion, and then find an energy provider with an output equivalent to 8 Hoover Dams. The same resources when devoted to mining honestly would be an extremely profitable enterprise. Such an attack is therefore economically irrational.

As of this writing, these things are true of quantum computing:

1. Quantum computers are extremely slow compared to conventional computers by many orders of magnitude.

2. Quantum computers are extremely expensive to build and will continue to be cost-prohibitive for quite some time.

3. The best-known quantum algorithms are a significant leap forward, but they would still require many billions of computers running for billions of years to crack the cryptography used in Bitcoin.

Even if scientists discovered new quantum algorithms that could break modern cryptography, quantum-safe cryptography would then be incorporated into Bitcoin.

In other words, Bitcoin's users and developer community would be able to stay one step ahead of any quantum attackers. While the Bitcoin community should be vigilant against large-scale attack possibilities, the average bitcoin user doesn't need to worry.

How can Bitcoin stay decentralized?

One of Bitcoin's most important properties is that anyone in the world can download a full copy of the entire Bitcoin ledger

— every single transaction ever made on the network — and verify for themselves that the historical record is correct.

As covered in Chapter 2, this practice is called running a *full node*. The ease of operating a full node is critical to the overall censorship-resistance of the Bitcoin network. If the Bitcoin network relied on a handful of companies or a small group of rich people to run full nodes, they could collude and edit the records, or steal coins. Each user can, by running a full node, verify everything and not have to trust anyone else. If expensive server equipment or fast internet connections were required to run a full node, this would force poorer people to trust others. The network would naturally centralize around first-world locations and high-tech businesses.

Fortunately, as the requirements to run a full node are very low, many thousands of users on different continents, completely unknown to each other, verify Bitcoin's blockchain on an ongoing basis. Moreover, with user-friendly hardware full nodes increasingly available on the market, operating a full node at home is accessible to non-technical users. Currently, several scientists at institutions like MIT and Stanford are helping to devise ways for anyone to run a full node on their mobile phone in the future, which would further improve the decentralization of the Bitcoin network.

Does Bitcoin protect privacy?

A popular misconception is that Bitcoin is anonymous. Bitcoin is pseudonymous and, with enough detective work and forensic analysis, a user's transactions and identity can be connected. With proper operational security, a savvy bitcoin user can disguise transactions to such an extent as to make surveillance difficult. With enough time or resources, however, a motivated nation-state or corporation can still track an individual down.

That said, bitcoin provides much better privacy for trans-actions than existing payment systems. Online purchases can be made with bitcoin without revealing private data such as someone's name, bank account, or address. That's an improve-ment over the existing banking system where governments, corporations, and merchants require and then share, sell, or leak private data on a daily basis.

Ongoing and scheduled improvements to Bitcoin, such as the Lightning Network, Taproot, Graftroot, and Schnorr Signa-tures, will collectively make private bitcoin transactions cheaper and easier. Bitcoin has the potential to be an excellent privacy technology, making mass financial surveillance extremely diffi-cult.

The internet was once completely open and public. As users and businesses required more private transactions, engineers added layers of privacy on top of the original internet. Private communication is now possible using apps that send automat-ically encrypted messages. Bitcoin is following a similar path.

How can Bitcoin meet the needs of 7 billion people?

In 1989, when scientists invented the World Wide Web to run on top of the internet, the idea that users could one day be exchanging photos, much less video, seemed technically impossible. As technology improved and evolved, the internet has scaled to accommodate once-unthinkable, resource-in-tensive applications like video sharing and conferencing. 300 hours of video are uploaded every minute to YouTube, and 5 billion videos are watched every day. Just like the internet, there are many ways to scale Bitcoin.

As discussed in Chapter 4, Bitcoin's capacities are currently being augmented through the Lightning Network. In addition to enhancing transaction privacy, Lightning also scales the Bitcoin network.

Lightning can handle millions of bitcoin transactions per second. Bitcoin is on track to scale exponentially, whereas traditional payment networks like Visa scale linearly by adding more and more servers. Bitcoin could revolutionize money and enable completely new products using micropayments as granular as one-one-thousandths (1/1000) satoshi at a time.

Through a combination of cautious, slow, ultra-secure and censorship-resistant occasional *on-chain* transactions, and batched, instantaneous, and cheap transactions on Lightning, Bitcoin can become a full-featured global payment system. This is a vision worth pursuing, as it would further take the power over finance out of the hands of governments and corporations and put it back in the hands of people.

Although hard to imagine today, Bitcoin meeting the needs of billions of people is no less of an outlandish concept than streaming video to billions of viewers once was on the internet.

Is there extreme wealth inequality in Bitcoin?

People who were involved with Bitcoin at an early stage did have the opportunity to accumulate a lot of Bitcoin. The blockchain, however, shows that many early adopters from 2009 to 2012 also sold their Bitcoin in the same time period. Many buyers at $1 in 2011 sold for $4 several months later or $30 a couple of months after that.

Many early adopters didn't have the stomach to ride through the extreme volatility and uncertainty of the early days, or lost their private keys, rendering their bitcoins permanently lost. Those that held on supported the ecosystem from its infancy and genuinely believe in Bitcoin's potential to change the world. Today, there are a few thousand addresses that store the majority of Bitcoin. Some are individuals who are now extremely rich. Most are companies that use such addresses to store the wealth of tens of thousands of their customers (i.e., Coinbase, Binance). As there's no one-to-one correlation between addresses and users, it is hard to tell exactly what the wealth distribution might be.

Bitcoin is not going to solve economic inequality. Anyone who says that is lying. However, as a universally accessible store of value that cannot be devalued by governments, Bitcoin gives savers a fair chance to keep what they earn as they get older, unlike the current monetary system.

If there are only 21 million bitcoins, how can the whole world use them?

Traditional fiat currency units are typically divided into 100 subunits called pennies or cents. USD and EUR can be divided into 100 cents, CNY into 10 jiao or 100 fen, and CZK (Czech koruna) into 100 haler.

Bitcoins, on the other hand, can be divided into 100,000,000 (one hundred million) smaller units. The atomic unit of bitcoin is called a called *satoshi* (or *sat*, for short) after the inventor of Bitcoin.

Thus, the total supply of bitcoin is 2,100,000,000,000,000 satoshis. For context, this is more divisible than the USD, whose M2 money supply is 1,500,000,000,000,000 cents as of this writing. The divisibility of bitcoin is on par or better than the USD.

As a thought exercise, dividing all existing satoshis among 7 billion people yields 300,000 sats per person. That seems like enough divisibility to satisfy the economic activities of each individual should bitcoin become the dominant money of the world.

How can I afford bitcoin? The price is so high!

Bitcoin is divisible, so it is possible to buy a small fraction of a bitcoin — $5 or $25 worth of bitcoin is currently equivalent to 0.00044 bitcoins and 0.0022 bitcoins, respectively.

How do I acquire bitcoins?

Primary ways to obtain bitcoin include:

1. Mining
2. Buying
3. Earning

Mining

At this point in Bitcoin's history, Bitcoin mining is a very low margin business. Much like gold mining, the equipment, industry contacts, and specialized knowledge to mine profitably require years of experience and millions of dollars in capital. As such, mining has become the domain of businesses and organizations with significant resources and knowhow, and it is infeasible for inexperienced individuals to mine profitably. For new users, bitcoin will be cheaper to acquire by buying or earning than mining.

Buying

There are several ways to buy bitcoin, some more private than others. Bitcoin ATMs and peer-to-peer trading are fast and relatively private.

Investors can sign up for online exchanges, many of which are listed in Additional Resources. New customers are required to submit their personal information, and the approval process takes anywhere from a few minutes to a few days. These companies act like banks and hold their customers' bitcoins and fiat in custody. Using them therefore involves giving up some privacy, but customers can ensure ownership of their bitcoins by withdrawing from these services to their personal wallets.

Earning

Using a Bitcoin or Lightning wallet, anyone can directly receive bitcoin as payment for goods or services. Employees can use Bitcoin payroll services to receive a portion of their wages in bitcoin instead of fiat.

How do I use a bitcoin wallet?

There are many different types of bitcoin wallets, including hardware wallets, desktop, mobile, and online wallets. Each have different security, convenience, and privacy trade-offs which users will want to study.

A reasonably secure way to store bitcoin is via a non-custodial wallet, which are listed under Hardware Wallets in Additional Resources. Meanwhile, the most convenient way to get started is to download a free mobile wallet, some of which are listed under Mobile Wallets in Additional Resources.

After downloading, the first step in setting up a Bitcoin wallet is to create a backup. This backup is referred to as a *seed phrase*, and is used to recreate the wallet should it get lost. The seed phrase is a list of words that is typically written on a piece of paper. Because a seed phrase can be used to recreate the wallet, it must be carefully secured. Think of this seed phrase in the same way as a gold bar or a diamond. The seed phrase has significant value and must be protected accordingly. As the ecosystem grows, new wallets have focused on decreasing complexity while improving usability, security, and privacy.

Once a wallet is set up, it can generate unique addresses for each new payment. This is different from the way usual banking payments work, where a customer is typically offered only one account number. Bitcoin brings better financial privacy by issuing unique addresses, all of which belong to the same bitcoin wallet.

As mentioned in the Why Have So Many Exchanges Been Hacked? section, investors using custodial services are subject to exchange hacking risk. Withdrawing funds to personal wallets after purchase will mitigate that risk.

Additional Resources

The Bitcoin Whitepaper

Bitcoin: A Peer-to-Peer Electronic Cash System by Satoshi Nakamoto is the original masterpiece that set the last ten years' worth of financial innovation in motion.

Source Code

Bitcoin Core is the source code for Bitcoin's reference full node software. Originally created by Satoshi Nakamoto, Bitcoin Core has contributions from over 500 developers around the world.

Books

The Internet of Money (Vol 1 & 2) by Andreas M. Antonopoulos is an in-depth dive into the "why" of Bitcoin in a series of his essays and talks.

Programming Bitcoin by Jimmy Song is a hands-on technical guide from one of the leading teachers on Bitcoin programming for developers interested in building with and contributing to the technology.

The Bitcoin Standard by Saifedean Ammous provides an economic history of money and an explanation of how Bitcoin provides an alternative to central banking.

Inventing Bitcoin by Yan Pritzker is a step-by-step walk-through how Bitcoin works, with nothing more than a high school level math background necessary.

Grokking Bitcoin by Kalle Rosenbaum is a fully illustrated guide to how Bitcoin works.

Bitcoin Money: A Tale of Bitville Discovering Good Money by The Bitcoin Rabbi is a children's book with colorful characters to help kids learn about Bitcoin.

Mastering Bitcoin: Programming the Open Blockchain by Andreas M. Antonopoulos is a comprehensive guide to programming for and with Bitcoin.

Websites & Publications

Bitcoin.org contains helpful information on how to get started, along with documentation and links to other resources. Using Bitcoin.com is not recommended, as the website intentionally conflates other cryptocurrencies with BTC in an attempt to get customers to buy them instead.

Bitcoin.page is a true treasure trove of educational resources and information about Bitcoin carefully curated by Jameson Lopp.

Bitcoin Wiki is a public resource for the community of Bitcoin users, developers, businesses, and anyone interested in Bitcoin.

Coin Center is a US-based non-profit focused on the policy issues facing Bitcoin and other cryptocurrencies. They constantly publish insightful plain-language explainers of various topics.

Bitcoinmining.com has resources on mining Bitcoin; how it works, getting started, and a list of hardware comparisons.

Global Coin Research focuses on cryptocurrency trends between the United States and Asia.

Podcasts

Tales from the Crypt is a podcast hosted by Marty Bent as he sits down to discuss Bitcoin with interesting people.

What Bitcoin Did is a twice-weekly show where Peter McCormack interviews leaders and influencers in the Bitcoin community.

The Stephan Livera Podcast is a podcast focused on educational interviews and discussions about the economics and technology of Bitcoin.

Noded is a podcast hosted by Michael Goldstein and Pierre Rochard focused on new technical developments on Bitcoin.

Off the Chain is a podcast by Anthony Pompliano exploring how investors from the new and old financial system are thinking about digital assets like Bitcoin.

Unchained and Unconfirmed are weekly podcasts where host Laura Shin interviews marquee names in cryptocurrency.

Let's Talk Bitcoin presents the ideas and people involved with cryptocurrency through a series of interviews and conversations with a group of regular hosts.

The Bitcoin Knowledge Podcast is a show where Trace Mayer interviews prominent contributors within the Bitcoin industry to help listeners better understand the technology.

Online Exchanges

Disclaimer: Although this section mentions specific sites, apps, or services within the Bitcoin ecosystem, this should not be construed as endorsements or investment advice. As with other parts of this book, the reader is encouraged to do their own research.

Fiat-to-Crypto

Bitfinex - Hong Kong based exchange started in 2014
CashApp - Square app for iOS and Android for buying bitcoin using a debit card
Kraken - US and EU exchange started in 2014

Crypto-to-Crypto

Binance - Malta-based exchange started in 2017
BitMex - Seychelles-based exchange started in 2014
Bittrex - US exchange started in 2016

Peer-to-Peer Marketplaces

LocalBitcoins - Finnish bitcoin marketplace started in 2012
Paxful - US bitcoin marketplace started in 2015
Bisq - A privacy-focused marketplace launched in 2014

Wallets

Custodial (customers do not control their private keys)

Blockchain.info
CashApp
Coinbase

Non-Custodial (customers control their private keys)

BreadWallet - iOS wallet
Bitcoin Core - Desktop wallet
Casa Keymaster - Android and iOS multisig app with
hardware wallet support
Samourai - Android wallet
Wasabi - Desktop wallet

Hardware (customers control their private keys)

ColdCard
Ledger
Trezor

Full Node Solutions

Casa Node - Plug&Play Lightning and Bitcoin full node
Nodl - Bitcoin and Lightning full node

Glossary

address - Similar to a bank account number, a bitcoin address is where bitcoin is received. Each address has a corresponding private key that allows the owner to spend the bitcoin by creating a digital signature.

bancor - the unit for a global currency proposed at Bretton Woods in 1944.

Bitcoin - a system of decentralized, digital, scarce money created by Satoshi Nakamoto.

bitcoin - the unit of value on the Bitcoin network. Each bitcoin is 100,000,000 satoshis.

block - a group of bitcoin transactions combined with a rare proof-of-work number. A block is equivalent to a page in Bitcoin's accounting ledger. A new block is created approximately every 10 minutes.

blockchain - a decentralized ledger system pioneered by Bitcoin. In Bitcoin, the blockchain tracks how much bitcoin there is in each address. The components of a blockchain are blocks.

blockchain technology - systems created to utilize Bitcoin's blockchain innovation in some capacity. There have not been any that have seen widespread adoption besides Bitcoin and a handful of other cryptocurrencies.

BTC - symbol/ticker used to represent bitcoin on exchanges, merchants and wallets. XBT is also a popular symbol.

central authority - an agency or organization that makes decisions for a given system.

centralized - a system with a single point of failure. This may be, for example, a system run by a person, foundation, company, or government.

crypto-to-crypto exchanges - an exchange that allows trading only between cryptocurrencies

decentralized - a system without a single point of failure.

digital signature - proof that the user, or signer, knows the private key of a given address. This is conceptually similar to signing a bank check to confirm that a given person is the account holder, but has the additional advantage of not actually needing to reveal the person's handwriting. When sending bitcoins, the sender signs the transaction, proving ownership of the bitcoin, without revealing the private key.

dollar standard - the system of monetary domination by USD in global trade. Started in 1944 after Bretton Woods and continued in 1971 through the petrodollar.

fiat currency - a currency that is issued by a central bank.

fiat-to-crypto exchanges - an exchange that allows trading of fiat directly to cryptocurrencies

FOMO - "Fear Of Missing Out," a term often used to describe herd mentality and irrational purchasing decisions.

full node - software used to validate the transactions and the integrity of the blockchain.

gold standard - a dominant world monetary system where the value of a nation's fiat currency was backed by an amount of gold which that government held in reserve.

halving - an event on the Bitcoin network where every 4 years, the mining reward in a block decreases by half.

KYC - "Know Your Customer," a practice enforced by governments where banks need to gather lots of personal information about someone in order to provide them a financial service. This information is then provided to governments through laws like the US Bank Secrecy Act.

leveraged exchanges - an exchange that allows trading up to 100 times the deposit amount

Lightning network - a system developed to scale the capacity of Bitcoin to millions of transactions per second. This innovation also adds significant privacy to Bitcoin transactions.

liquidity - the amount of an asset that is easily bought or sold in a given period

miner - an individual or a group (called "mining pools") that use specialized computers to find rare proof-of-work numbers in order to create new blocks.

mining reward / miner fee - the bitcoins a miner receives for processing transactions and securing the Bitcoin network.

Octopus card - an electronic payment card in Hong Kong.

off-chain transaction - a transaction that is not recorded in the Bitcoin blockchain, as is the case with Lightning network transactions.

on-chain transaction - a transaction that is processed and recorded directly in the Bitcoin blockchain.

peer-to-peer exchanges - an exchange that requires meeting in person to execute a trade

private key - similar to a password to a bank account, a private key unlocks the ability to transfer bitcoins from a given wallet. Ownership of the private keys is therefore the same as owning the bitcoins.

proof-of-work - the process by which miners prove that they have expended energy to propose a new valid block that may be added to the blockchain.

public blockchain - a blockchain that can be downloaded, accessed, and browsed by anyone.

sat / satoshi - the smallest unit of bitcoin. 100,000,000 satoshis is 1 bitcoin.

Satoshi Nakamoto - the creator of Bitcoin.

wallet - an app or a hardware device which allows users to send and receive bitcoins.

whitepaper - an authoritative, often academic, report intended to fully inform the reader on a particular topic. The original document describing Bitcoin and its technical details were presented in this format in October 2008 by Satoshi Nakamoto.

Acknowledgments

Acknowledgments

The authors would like to thank the following people for lending their time and expertise to what would otherwise have been a far more challenging undertaking:

Leigh Cuen
Sam Corcos
Nick Foley
Irl Nathan
Jane Song Lee
June Park
Rodrigo Linares
Jan Čapek
Nick Neuman
Tomiwa Lasebikan

We would also like to thank the following individuals for supporting us during our book sprint:

Bill Barhydt
Daniel Buchner
Cryptograffiti
Jill Carlson
Juan Gutiérrez
Han Hua
Ben Richman
Bill Tai
Mike Youssefmir
Sebastien Lhuilieri

The following individuals have both informed and inspired us throughout the years:

Nick Szabo
Andreas Antonopoulos

Jameson Lopp
Elizabeth Stark
Marek Palatinus
Pavol Rusnak
Michelle Lai

The following organizations encouraged us to write this book:

Blockchain Capital
BloomX
BuyCoins Africa
Casa
Human Rights Foundation
Open Money Initiative
University of Texas

And of course, we are very grateful to Tim Chang for letting us use his wonderful home, and most importantly, our families and loved ones for cheering us on.